THE
POCKET BOOK
OF
CHELSEA

By Clive Batty

Published by Vision Sports Publishing in 2010

Vision Sports Publishing
19-23 High Street
Kingston upon Thames
Surrey
KT1 1LL

www.visionsp.co.uk

Text © Clive Batty
Illustrations © Bob Bond
Sporting Caricatures

ISBN: 978-1905326-93-8

Series editor: Jim Drewett
Series production: Martin Cloake
Design: Neal Cobourne
Illustrations: Bob Bond
Cover photography: Paul Downes, Objective Image
All pictures: Getty Images

Printed and bound in China by Toppan Printing Co Ltd

A CIP catalogue record for this book is available from the British Library

THIS IS AN UNOFFICIAL PUBLICATION

All statistics in *The Pocket Book of Chelsea* are correct up until the end of the 2009/10 season.

CONTENTS

FOREWORD BY

KERRY DIXON

In the summer of 1983 I had just finished the season as the top scorer in the Third Division with Reading. Quite a few clubs, including Sheffield Wednesday, Coventry and Watford, were keen to sign me. Chelsea, who were then in the Second Division, were also in the hunt. As a kid I'd seen the 1970 FA Cup final between Chelsea and Leeds and it was one of those wonderful finals where the underdog beats the favourite. That game was one of the reasons I chose to go to Chelsea. It wasn't a difficult decision, really. Out of all the clubs who were interested in me, Chelsea was the sleeping giant. At the same time, I still believed that Chelsea was a top club and I wanted to be part of getting them back to where they belonged.

It couldn't have gone any better, particularly in the first few years, and through my exploits with Chelsea I realised a childhood dream to play for England. I had nine wonderful years at Chelsea and ended up as the club's second highest ever scorer. To finish just short of the all-time record was a bit galling, but there was something symbolic about it: nine years wearing the number nine shirt and nine goals away from the record!

These days I work for Chelsea in corporate hospitality on match days and often get invited to appear on Chelsea TV. I really enjoy being around the club and mixing with the fans, who always give me a fantastic reception. Some of the ex-players I regularly bump into at the Bridge, like Peter Bonetti and Ron Harris, are featured among the legends in the 'Hall of Fame' section in this book, and rightly so. These lists always produce debate and some fans might be disappointed that, say, Ruud Gullit or Gianluca Vialli have been left out. I would say, though, that they were superstars who played for the club for a relatively short time rather than real 'Chelsea legends' who spent all or most of their careers at the Bridge.

Reading about the 1984 Chelsea-Leeds match in the 'Great Games' section brought back some wonderful memories for me. After a great season for myself and the club this was the game that got Chelsea back in the big time. Over 30,000 fans saw us put on a fantastic performance to beat Leeds 5-0, and for me personally to score a hat-trick was just brilliant. At the final whistle thousands of fans poured onto the pitch to celebrate promotion, and to see the elation and joy on their faces made it a really special day.

I think any Chelsea fan would enjoy reading this great book, which is packed with information about the Blues. From the history of the club through the various ages to some of the individual Chelsea heroes, the great games, the most memorable goals, the different kits and the recording of 'Blue is the Colour'...it's all in here!

...CLUB DIRECTORY...

Club address: Chelsea Football Club
Stamford Bridge
Fulham Road
London
SW6 1HS

General club enquiries: 0871 984 1955

Ticket sales: 0871 984 1905 (UK)
0207 835 6000 (International)

Membership: 0871 984 1905

Stadium Megastore: 0871 984 1955

Online Megastore: (www.chelseamegastore.com):
0871 231 0005

Stadium & Museum tours: 0871 984 1955

Chelsea TV (Sky Digital): 0870 580 0803

Chelsea TV (Homechoice): 0800 072 3363

CHELSEA v JUVENTUS
Stamford Bridge Stadium
Wednesday, 25 February 2009   Kick Off 19:45
WEST STAND LOWER
GATE:8 ROW:2   SEAT:0203

Chelsea Pitch Owners: 01932 851488

Football in the Community soccer schools:

0207 957 8220

(London/Essex)

01932 596139

(Surrey/Sussex)

Chelsea Old Boys: 0207 957 8261

Past Players' Trust: 0207 958 2881

Chelsea programme/official magazine:

0207 293 3000

Marco restaurant: 0207 915 2929

Frankie's Sports Bar and Grill:

0207 957 8298

Club website: www.chelseafc.com

FRANK LAMPAR

· MIDFIELDER ·

CHELSEA

Peter Osgood
CENTRE FORWARD

CHELSEA
FOOTBALL CLUB
AUTOGLASS
OFFICIAL CLUB SPONSOR

SEASON TICKET
CF BATTY

017298

mbership Office for conditions of use.

STORY OF THE BLUES
THE EARLY DAYS
1905-39

In 1904 Gus Mears, a London business contractor, and his brother Joseph bought the freehold to Stamford Bridge, then operating as an athletics stadium. Their dream was to create the finest sporting arena in the country, with football topping the bill. After Fulham turned down an offer to move into the stadium, the brothers decided to form a new club with the aim of applying for membership of the Southern League. Kensington FC, London FC and Stamford Bridge FC were all discussed as possible names before the new club was christened Chelsea FC.

In March 1905 the club appointed John Tait Robertson, a 28-year-old Scottish international half-back, as player/manager on wages of £4 per week. The following month Chelsea applied for membership of the Football League, Tottenham and Fulham having opposed the entry of another London club into the Southern League. By the time of the Football League AGM on 29th May 1905 Chelsea had signed up a full squad of players, including William 'Fatty' Foulke, a 22-stone goalkeeper from Sheffield United.

Chelsea's representative at the AGM, Frederick Parker, made a compelling case for the club to be elected to the League. Given just three minutes to talk, he made three simple but effective points: first, that the club was financially stable; second, he emphasised that the Bridge met all the League's stadium requirements; and third, he read out the full

list of players who were contracted to the club. He
ended his speech by saying, "You will come to the
conclusion that you cannot really refuse us!" He was
right. The club were elected to the Second Division
without having kicked a ball.

On 2nd September 1905 Chelsea played their
first ever Football League fixture, losing 1-0 away
to Stockport County. The new boys got their first
taste of victory a week later at Blackpool, Robertson
getting the only goal, and two days after that 6,000
fans turned up to witness the club's first competitive
home fixture, a 5-1 thrashing of Hull. Chelsea finished
the season in third place, 13 points behind Second

Chelsea FC in 1905.
Giant captain and
goalkeeper William
'Fatty' Foulke is easy to
pick out in the back row

Division champions Manchester United, whose visit
to the Bridge on Good Friday attracted a massive
crowd of 67,000 to the Bridge. The potential of the
new club was there for all to see.

The following season Chelsea won promotion
to the First Division, new striker George 'Gatling

Gun' Hilsdon contributing 27 goals. Now managed by David Calderhead, a low-key character dubbed the 'Chelsea Sphinx' who would remain at the helm until 1933, the club stayed in the top flight for just three seasons before being relegated. Nonetheless, the crowds still flocked to the Bridge, the average home attendance of 28,545 being the highest in the country in 1909/10 despite the club's demotion.

An artist's impression of Chelsea scoring against Spurs in 1909

Chelsea were back in the First Division, although struggling in the relegation zone, when they reached the FA Cup final for the first time in 1915. With trench warfare raging across the Channel, the venue for the match was switched from Crystal Palace to Old Trafford in an effort to reduce absenteeism from essential war work. Just two trains travelled up from London, leaving Chelsea fans very much in a minority, the crowd being largely made up of Blades supporters and soldiers in uniform. Disappointingly, Chelsea slumped to a 3-0 defeat in a one-sided affair. Four days later a 2-0 defeat at Notts County confirmed Chelsea's relegation back to the Second Division.

When football resumed after the end of the First World War, however, Chelsea were still in the top flight, the club earning a reprieve when the First Division was expanded from 20 to 22 teams. The Londoners took full advantage of the let-off, finishing third in the league and reaching the semi-final of the FA Cup in 1920, thanks in part to the goals of striker Jack Cock, a £2,500 recruit from Huddersfield.

As a whole, though, the 1920s were a desperately disappointing decade for Chelsea. After narrowly avoiding relegation in 1923, the Pensioners splashed out a club record £6,500 on Middlesbrough's Scottish international playmaker Andy Wilson, only for both clubs to go down at the end of the season. Chelsea fans then endured a number of frustrating campaigns as the club seemed certain to get back to the big time, only to be foiled at the last. Finally, after six long years in the wilderness, the Pensioners won promotion in 1930, young striker George Mills scoring some vital goals after breaking into the team just before Christmas.

Determined to put their yo-yo years behind them, Chelsea spent lavishly on their return to the top flight. Heading the list of high profile signings were three Scottish internationals: prolific centre forward Hughie Gallacher, who arrived from Newcastle for a club record £10,000; Huddersfield winger Alex Jackson, like Gallacher a member of the famous

'Wembley Wizards' Scotland side that had thrashed England 5-1 in 1928; and Alex Cheyne, a £6,000 recruit from Aberdeen who was renowned for his ability to score direct from corners.

On the first day of training at Stamford Bridge in 1935, the players muck in by building the goals

The Londoners were the talk of the football world, but their expensively-assembled team failed to set the league alight. For most of the 1930s Chelsea were mired in mid-table, rising to the heady heights of eighth in 1936. The FA Cup offered greater hopes of glory, but a semi-final defeat by Newcastle in 1932 ensured that the club's trophy cabinet would remain disappointingly bare. Even a new manager, former Manchester City and Arsenal boss Leslie Knighton arriving in 1933, failed to improve the team's fortunes. Yet, with huge crowds continuing to pack out the Bridge – a then Football League record of 82,905 attending the home derby with Arsenal in October 1935 – the lack of silverware seemed to matter little to the fans.

By the time the Second World War brought a premature end to the 1939/40 season Chelsea were firmly established as a top-flight club known for their entertaining style of play, massive support and ability to spend big in the transfer market, but far too inconsistent to be considered genuine contenders. It would be an image that the club would find devilishly difficult to shake off.

Some of the 82,905 people who packed into the Bridge for the visit of London neighbours Arsenal in 1935

BADGE OF
HONOUR

Nothing, it seems, lasts for ever at Chelsea, a club that has always been associated with change and innovation. Even the club badge has been through a number of radical redesigns, the current crest being the fifth to be officially adopted by the club.

In 1905, when Chelsea FC was founded, the club decided on the image of a cheery Chelsea Pensioner complete with full white beard and row of military medals as its badge. Given the name of the club the choice was an obvious one, while the fact that the Chelsea Pensioners had a history in the local area stretching back to 1692, when their home at the Royal Hospital was opened, would also have worked in their favour. Although the logo did not appear on the team's shirts it did feature in the match programme and, inevitably, the club were soon nicknamed 'the Pensioners' – a moniker which proved to be a godsend to music hall comedians, especially as the club's early decades were hardly awash with glory.

The cheery Pensioner of the club's first badge

The jokes, though, certainly didn't amuse Ted Drake, the former Arsenal and England striker who became Chelsea manager in 1952. As part of his efforts to modernise the club's image he banished the Chelsea Pensioner from the club badge and decided

The stop-gap badge adopted in 1952...

on a new nickname, 'the Blues'. While a new badge was being designed, a stop-gap logo consisting of the club's 'CFC' initials was used for the 1952/53 season.

Inspired by the civic coat of arms of the Metropolitan Borough of Chelsea, the new crest featured a rampant lion holding a staff. The lion was derived from the arms of the Earl of Cadogan, who held the title of Viscount Chelsea and was also president of the club, while the staff was that of the Bishop of Westminster whose jurisdiction extended over Chelsea. This classic badge was first sewn onto the players' shirts in 1960 but the complexity of the design meant several simplified variations were stitched into the shirts at later points of the decade. Indeed, for a while in the mid-1960s the club opted simply for a squiggly 'CFC' logo before the lion made a roaring return to the shirts in 1967. When, three years later, Chelsea won the FA Cup for

...gave way to the classic Chelsea lion

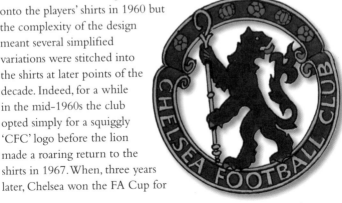

the first time a symbol of the trophy appeared on the shirts alongside the badge, to be replaced by two stars when a second piece of silverware, the European Cup Winners' Cup, was added to the Stamford Bridge trophy cabinet in 1971.

The badge became one of the most instantly recognisable in English football but in 1986 new chairman Ken Bates, advised that he did not hold copyright in the existing crest, replaced it with a non-heraldic, more naturalistic lion standing over the club's initials. Chelsea supporters were largely unimpressed by the new design, many feeling that it looked far too similar for their liking to the badge of despised London rivals Millwall.

Charlie Cooke sports the classic Chelsea badge in 1968, before any stars were added

A long-running fans' campaign to have the old Chelsea badge restored was ignored until Russian billionaire Roman Abramovich bought the club from Bates in 2003. The following year, to much fanfare, the club unveiled a new crest created by the London design company Blue Dog. A contemporary reworking of the 1953-86 badge, it first appeared on the players' shirts during the club's centenary season in 2005/06, the anniversary being marked by a special gold version of the crest. Then manager Jose Mourinho was among those to be impressed by the new design, remarking at the launch: "When I look to this lion, it looks arrogant, it is aggressive, it is powerful. He is proud of being a Chelsea lion. For me, for my players, and for the people working with me who feel the responsibility of winning, I think this badge will make us even more aware of our ambition." Fans, too, were delighted to see the back of the 'Bates badge' and the return of the bold, upright lion with its associations with the club's first glorious era in the 1970s.

Chelsea have stated that the current badge will remain on the players' shirts for the next 100 years. Time will tell but, given the changes to the club crest over the previous century, few would bet on it.

Left: The infamous 'Bates badge'

The modern badge, which the club say will last 100 years

DOUBLE DELIGHT

A last blast of referee Chris Foy's whistle at Wembley on 15th May 2010 signalled that Chelsea had not only retained the FA Cup for the first time in their history but, even more significantly, claimed a first ever league and cup Double. To the delight of their legions of fans, the Blues' season had ended in complete triumph with the Londoners joining an elite group of clubs to have won the English game's two most important domestic honours in the same season. What's more, they had achieved this success in some style, playing attractive, entertaining football and setting numerous records along the way.

For manager Carlo Ancelotti, only installed in the Bridge hotseat a year earlier after leaving AC Milan, the two trophies represented a clear vindication of his calm, clear-headed approach during the season, his first in English football. Ignoring the many critics, including Manchester United manager Sir Alex Ferguson, who had labelled the Chelsea squad 'too old' Ancelotti put his faith in seasoned players rather than adding new faces to the team. He believed Didier Drogba, Frank Lampard and Michael Ballack all still had plenty to offer despite being the wrong side of 30. As it turned out, the Italian's decision to go with the players he had inherited proved to be a wise one.

With his vast experience of the tactically intricate Italian game, Ancelotti was never likely to struggle when it came to setting out his team in an effective playing

Chelsea's Double-winners paint the town blue

system. After starting the season with a diamond midfield formation which didn't quite hit the hoped for heights, the Italian experimented with a couple of different systems before settling on an attacking 4-3-3 line up in the closing months of the season. It worked a treat as the Blues won seven of their last eight league games, scoring an impressive 33 goals in the process.

Although Chelsea finished the campaign just one point ahead of runners-up Manchester United there was no doubt that the Blues were worthy champions. For a start, they had shown they had the upper hand over the Reds in their two face-to-face meetings, beating them 1-0 at Stamford Bridge before Christmas thanks to a headed goal by skipper John Terry, then winning a crucial encounter in April at Old Trafford 2-1, with goals by Joe Cole and Drogba.

Then, there were the remarkable goalscoring feats Ancelotti's free-flowing side accomplished. Needing just a win at home against Wigan on the last day of the season to be certain of clinching the title, the Blues went goal-crazy, hammering the Latics 8-0. As shot after shot bulged the net, the records tumbled: when Salomon Kalou rifled in the third, Chelsea became the highest ever scorers in a Premiership season; when Drogba scored the fifth, Chelsea became the first club since Tottenham in 1962/63 to hit a century of goals in the top flight; and when Ashley Cole joyfully volleyed home the eighth goal in the final minute, the Blues bumped up their goal difference to 71, the best ever for a top-flight campaign. Drogba's hat-trick in the same game, meanwhile, ensured that he comfortably beat Wayne Rooney in the race for the Golden Boot.

Drogba and Terry lead the cheers

The players celebrated their title success with a night out in glitzy Mayfair, but they were soon back on the training pitch at Cobham, preparing for the FA Cup final against Portsmouth the next weekend. Relegated from the Premier League and in dire financial straits, Pompey were expected to be simply making up the numbers at Wembley, but they proved to be obdurate opponents. True, Chelsea hit the post or bar five times in the first half and might easily have had the game won by the break, but it was Portsmouth who had the best chance to open the scoring early in the second half when they were awarded a penalty. However, Kevin-Prince Boateng's kick was weak and Petr Cech was able to save with his legs. Minutes later, Chelsea took full advantage of their let-off, Drogba curling home a free-kick past Pompey keeper David James. Although the normally reliable Lampard missed a penalty late on, it mattered little – the cup, and the fabled Double, were Chelsea's.

A Chelsea fan celebrates the fact that nothing stopped his side

"We have to celebrate this victory together because everyone put something in for winning this Double," said Ancelotti afterwards. The very next day the team did exactly that, showing off their newly-won silverware from an open-top bus in front of thousands of ecstatic fans lining the streets around Stamford Bridge. All in all, the perfect end to a memorable season.

CHELSEA
COMIC STRIP HISTORY
1

IN 1971 CHELSEA THRASHED LUXEMBOURG PART-TIMERS JEUNESSE HAUTCHARAGE 13-0 IN THE CUP WINNERS' CUP AT STAMFORD BRIDGE... THEIR BIGGEST EVER WIN.

CHEL-SEA!

THE MINNOWS WERE NOT THE MOST ATHLETIC BUNCH... ONE OF THEIR PLAYERS HAD ONLY ONE ARM WHILE ANOTHER WORE GLASSES ON THE PITCH!

BLUES STRIKER PETER OSGOOD PARTICULARLY ENJOYED HIMSELF, SCORING FIVE OF HIS TEAM'S GOALS. THE 21-0 AGGREGATE SCORE IS A EUROPEAN RECORD TO THIS DAY...

THE BRIDGE

Stamford Bridge was officially opened on 28th April 1877 and for the next 28 years it was used almost exclusively as an arena for athletics by the London Athletic Club. In 1904 local businessmen Gus and Joseph Mears obtained the deeds and the following year, after Fulham had rejected an offer to move to the Bridge, they formed Chelsea FC.

A vast bowl with an opening capacity of nearly 70,000, the stadium was the second largest venue in England after Crystal Palace. As well as Chelsea home games, the ground hosted rugby league and union matches, while the track encircling the pitch was regularly used for athletics, speedway and greyhound racing.

In the 1980s, Chelsea's future at Stamford Bridge was thrown into grave doubt when the freehold of the stadium was taken over by property developers. However, the stadium was saved and completely redeveloped in the 1990s, the old terraces replaced by modern all-seater stands.

Above: An artist's impression of Stamford Bridge in the early years...

... and, right, the imposing modern arena of today

EAST STAND

Now the oldest part of the stadium, the East Stand
remains the most important part of the ground, housing
as it does the dug-outs, the tunnel, the dressing-rooms
and the press box.

Opened in 1974 with a capacity of 12,000, the
massive cantilevered three-tiered stand was the largest
in the country at the time. Its imposing framework,
constructed in self-weathering 'cor-ten' steel, earned
plaudits from architectural critics but its narrow
concourses, tight turnstile entrances and steep staircases
were not popular with fans. More importantly, the stand
cost twice the original estimate of £1 million, plunging
Chelsea deep into debt which took the club many years
to pay off.

While the Bridge was being redeveloped in the

*The Bridge staged FA
Cup finals between
1920 and 1922. Here
the vast stadium stands
empty on the morning
of the 1920 game*

mid-1990s, the lower tier of the stand was used to accommodate away fans. However, then Chelsea boss Jose Mourinho disliked having visiting supporters alongside the pitch and in 2005 they were banished to the Shed End.

The original East Stand was built in 1905, in the same year that Chelsea FC was formed, and seated 5,000 fans. It was designed by Archibald Leitch, a noted football stadium architect of the era who had previously overseen the construction of stands at Craven Cottage, Celtic Park, Ibrox and Hampden Park.

WEST STAND

Opened at the start of the 2001/02 season, the stand cost £30 million and houses 13,500 fans. It consists of three huge tiers, all with clear sightlines of the pitch,

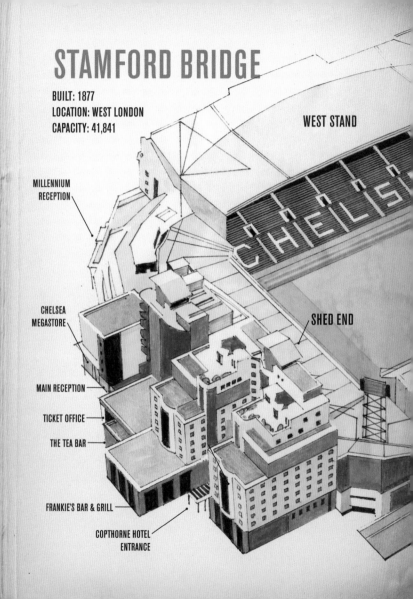

STAMFORD BRIDGE

BUILT: 1877
LOCATION: WEST LONDON
CAPACITY: 41,841

WEST STAND

MILLENNIUM
RECEPTION

CHELSEA
MEGASTORE

SHED END

MAIN RECEPTION

TICKET OFFICE

THE TEA BAR

FRANKIE'S BAR & GRILL

COPTHORNE HOTEL
ENTRANCE

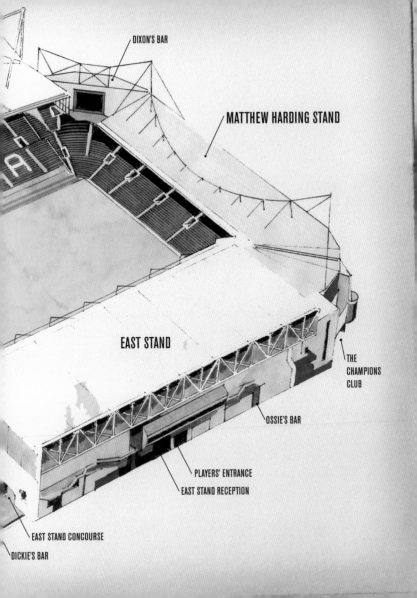

DIXON'S BAR

MATTHEW HARDING STAND

EAST STAND

THE CHAMPIONS CLUB

OSSIE'S BAR

PLAYERS' ENTRANCE

EAST STAND RECEPTION

EAST STAND CONCOURSE

DICKIE'S BAR

The old North Stand packed to the rafters during the visit of the great Moscow Dynamo in 1945 which attracted 82,000 spectators

plus a row of executive boxes that run the full length of the stand. The seats in the middle and upper tiers are the most expensive in the ground and are generally filled by well-heeled fans, among them Chelsea owner Roman Abramovich who watches most home games from the directors' box. Facilities inside the stand include six swish corporate hospitality suites named after former players and, on the ground floor, a large business venue.

The old West Stand stood from 1966-97 and featured a plain, column-supported roof over 6,300 tip-up seats with rows of basic concrete benches at the front seating a further 2,750 fans. The original plan for the stand included a car park on the roof but this bizarre notion was never pursued. Previously, the west side of Stamford Bridge consisted simply of banked terracing, originally formed using soil and clay which had been excavated from the construction of the Piccadilly tube line.

MATTHEW HARDING STAND

Opened as the North Stand in 1994, the lower tier in particular has since become the home of the Blues' most vocal fans. With a capacity of over 10,000 the two-tiered stand has a vast roof and provides excellent, unobstructed views from all seats. A big screen is attached to the roof on the western side, one of two inside the ground.

Around two-thirds of the stand's £7.5million costs were put up in form of loan stock by Matthew Harding, a wealthy Chelsea fan with a background in insurance. In 1996 the stand was renamed after its benefactor, following Harding's death in a helicopter crash while he was travelling back from a Chelsea away match.

The original 2,500-capacity North Stand, on which work began in 1939 before it was completed after the Second World War, rose above the terracing on stilts in the north-east corner next to the East Stand and was built with greyhound race-goers in mind as much as

football fans. Situated near the railway line behind
Stamford Bridge, the stand vibrated when trains
passed at speed and, shortly before it was demolished
in 1973, it was closed on safety grounds.

For two decades afterwards the area was left
as uncovered, increasingly crumbling, terracing.
For many years it accommodated away fans who,
depending on their numbers, either occupied the
whole end or were corralled in a pen in the north-
eastern corner.

SHED END

Completed in 1997 in a style similar to the earlier
North Stand, the two-tiered Shed End stand has a
capacity of slightly under 7,000. The smallest stand at
the Bridge, its size was limited by Chelsea chairman
Ken Bates's decision to build a hotel, restaurants and
health club directly behind it as part of the Chelsea
Village complex.

The stand's name comes from the legendary terrace
which became the preferred vantage point for the
club's younger, more vocal, scarf-waving fans in the
1960s. Known to supporters as 'The Shed', a reference
to the roof which was built in 1935 primarily to
keep bookies dry on greyhound nights, the terrace
was one of the most notorious in the country in
the hooligan-blighted 1970s and 1980s. The terrace
was demolished in 1994 and initially replaced with a
temporary uncovered stand before work began on the
new structure.

Lacoste, wedge
haircuts and the
Chelsea West Stand
– it could only be
the 1980s

GREAT GOALS

PETER OSGOOD
1970 FA CUP FINAL
REPLAY v LEEDS

With just 12 minutes left of the 1970 FA Cup final replay at Old Trafford, Chelsea were trailing 1-0 to Leeds and desperately searching for an equaliser.

Then, Blues' striker Ian Hutchinson picked up the ball in midfield before allowing Charlie Cooke, running towards him, to take possession. The Scottish international looked up and, noticing Peter Osgood's run from deep towards the far post, floated a diagonal cross from the right over and beyond the Leeds defence. The ball was perfectly delivered for Osgood who, having lost marker Jack Charlton, flung himself full length to head powerfully past Leeds goalkeeper David Harvey. The goal proved to be a turning point in the match for the Blues, who went on to lift the cup for the first time after defender David Webb scored the winner in extra-time.

"I was just there waiting for it in loads of space," recalled Osgood later. "David Harvey stayed on his line and that just gave me time to have a quick look at him and glance it the right way. I honestly thought I was offside, but I looked across and the linesman didn't have his flag up. I ran to our fans and I had goose pimples on my skin and the hairs on the back of my neck were standing on end. It was an incredible feeling."

ROBERTO DI MATTEO
1997 FA CUP FINAL v MIDDLESBROUGH

Chasing a first major honour for 26 years, Ruud Gullit's Blues got off to a sensational start with a magnificent goal in the first minute of the 1997 FA Cup final against Middlesbrough.

Deep in his own half, Chelsea skipper Dennis Wise dispossessed Boro's Phil Stamp before playing a simple pass to Roberto Di Matteo. The Italian midfielder carried the ball forward over the halfway line unchallenged. The Middlesbrough defence retreated, wary of the threat posed by other Chelsea players breaking in support. But Di Matteo didn't need any help: from 30 yards out, he unleashed a ferocious shot which flashed over Boro keeper Ben Roberts before going in off the underside of the crossbar. The strike was timed at just 43 seconds, the fastest ever goal in a Wembley cup final. Chelsea went on to win the match 2-0, Eddie Newton adding a second seven minutes from time.

"I thought to myself maybe I will shoot," Di Matteo revealed to the Chelsea FC magazine *Onside* soon after the final whistle. "So I did. I was very lucky because when I hit the ball it went first up and then down behind the goalkeeper. It was so quick, after that I was so excited. I was so carried away I just couldn't calm down and it was unbelievable, the feeling."

DI MATTEO

WISE

GUS POYET
1999 PREMIERSHIP
v SUNDERLAND

On the opening day of the 1999/2000 season Chelsea served up a treat for their supporters, thrashing Premiership newcomers Sunderland 4-0 at the Bridge.

While the Blues' performance as a whole was exceptional, the highlight of the match was the fourth goal by Gus Poyet.

Just a minute after Tore Andre Flo had given the Blues an unassailable 3-0 lead, Marcel Desailly played a short pass to new signing Didier Deschamps. From deep inside the Chelsea half, the Frenchman struck a long pass to Gianfranco Zola, who created space for himself by flicking the ball back over his head while Sunderland's players retreated towards their own goal. Surrounded by opponents and with only Flo up in support, his options still appeared limited. Looking around him, the little Italian maestro spotted Poyet's run into the box from deep and cleverly improvised a scooped pass over a trio of Black Cats. The ball fell perfectly for the Uruguayan midfielder, who lashed a thumping scissor-kick volley high into the net from around the penalty spot. The goal, which combined superb team play and brilliant execution, was one of the best at the Bridge for many a year.

"It was a magnificent finish," was Zola's post-match assessment. "It is not often you see a goal like that, which has finishing, passing, everything."

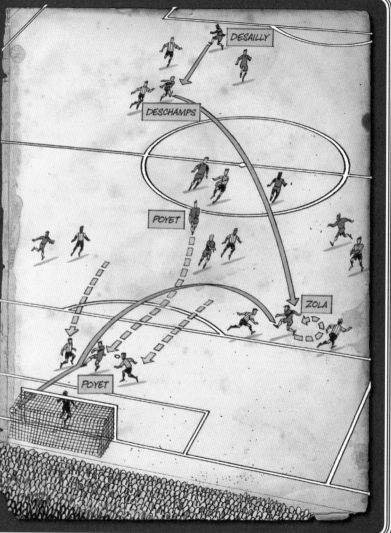

DENNIS WISE
1999 CHAMPIONS LEAGUE GROUP STAGE v AC MILAN

Still celebrated in song by Blues fans a decade after he scored it, Dennis Wise's equaliser against Italian giants AC Milan in the San Siro in 1999 is one of the most famous Chelsea goals ever.

Around 13 minutes of an absorbing Champions League fixture were left to play when Blues' left-back Celestine Babayaro played a low pass up the line to Tore Andre Flo. The Norwegian striker passed inside to substitute Roberto di Matteo, who initially miscontrolled the ball in midfield. However, the ball broke kindly for the Italian who immediately looked up and, spotting Wise's forward run, hit a magnificent 30-yard lofted pass over three Milan defenders straight into the Chelsea midfielder's path. Controlling the ball on his right foot, Wise powered into the penalty area before hitting a low left-foot shot through the legs of the advancing Milan goalkeeper, Christian Abbiati, and into the far corner of the goal.

"Robbie played the perfect ball into my path and I just had to make sure I took a good touch – which I did," recalled an excited Wisey afterwards. "Then I just thought 'I've got to keep it low' and I struck it. I knew it was in as soon as I hit it. It was great, just wonderful to score in the San Siro!"

GIANFRANCO ZOLA
2002 FA CUP THIRD ROUND REPLAY v NORWICH

If a single split second summed up the captivating genius of Gianfranco Zola it was this amazing piece of improvisation against Norwich at the Bridge in January 2002.

The Blues were already 2-0 up in their FA Cup third round replay when Graeme Le Saux rifled in a low right-wing corner. Running towards the near post, Zola jumped and, connecting perfectly with the ball, sent it into the net with an audacious backheel volley.

It all happened so quickly the crowd only really appreciated what they had witnessed when the goal was replayed on the stadium's giant screens. A collective gasp of amazement was followed by thunderous applause as fans at the Bridge finally realised that they had seen one of the all-time great goals.

"Don't ask me how I did it because I don't know," Zola modestly said afterwards. "I would be a liar if I said I wanted to do that. The only way I could score was with my right foot because with the left I can't do anything. It was one you try 100 times and it doesn't go in."

Zola may have tried to downplay his majestic moment, but his manager was having none of it. "This goal was fantasy, magic," beamed Claudio Ranieri. "Only Maradona, Pele, the big players, can do this. He's a wizard."

ZOLA

ZOLA

LE SAUX

EIDUR GUDJOHNSEN
2003 PREMIERSHIP
v LEEDS

A key member of the Chelsea team that won consecutive Premiership titles in 2005 and 2006, Eidur Gudjohnsen scored many brilliant goals for the Blues. But none better than this incredible bicycle kick against old rivals Leeds United.

The Blues were trailing 1-0 when Frank Lampard received a simple pass from Jody Morris just inside the Leeds half. Surging forward past two opponents, Lampard carried the ball out to the right wing before delivering a high cross towards Gudjohnsen, who was lurking near the penalty spot. The ball dropped a little behind the Icelandic striker who, showing remarkable confidence and technique, launched himself in the air to send a spectacular overhead kick beyond Leeds goalkeeper Paul Robinson and into the bottom corner of the goal.

"As soon as I connected I knew it was going to be a goal," Gudjohnsen said after the match, which Chelsea went on to win 3-2. "As a player, you never forget a goal like that."

Among the many plaudits Gudjohnsen received for his sensational strike was one from former Blues star Duncan McKenzie, an overhead kick specialist himself back in the 1970s. "The Gudjohnsen strike was as good a goal as I've seen in my whole life," he enthused. "I was brought up on Pele and Rivelino, but I can tell you that beat the lot."

DIDIER DROGBA
2006 PREMIERSHIP
v EVERTON

Deadly inside the penalty box, Didier Drogba has also always been capable of striking from distance – as he proved with this stunning 30-yard effort against Everton at Goodison Park in December 2006.

The Blues and the Toffees were tied at 2-2 with just a couple of minutes to play when Chelsea goalkeeper Hilario launched a long drop-kick downfield. Andriy Shevchenko headed the ball on to Drogba who controlled it on his chest, turning to face the Everton goal as he did so.

As the ball bounced up off the ground, Drogba unleashed a powerful, curving shot that dipped over Tim Howard in the Everton goal before smashing into the net. The goal proved to be the winner, completing a magnificent Blues comeback from 2-1 down in the final ten minutes, and Drogba celebrated it in some style by sliding on the wet turf towards the jubilant Chelsea fans.

After the match, Drogba's team-mates queued up to pay tribute to the Ivorian striker's marvellous piece of skill. "The vision and accuracy needed to shoot from there was unbelievable," reckoned full back Ashley Cole. Non-playing substitute Paulo Ferreira was equally impressed by Drogba's bolt from the blue. "It was a great goal," said the Portuguese defender. "The shot, the curve that the ball makes, it was unbelievable."

BLUE IS THE COLOUR

Although it was recorded nearly 40 years ago, *Blue is the Colour* remains an essential and much-loved part of the pre-match build-up at Stamford Bridge. No more so than on Champions League nights, when opera singer Stuart Pendred strides out onto the pitch to lead the crowd in a full-throated rendition of the club anthem while twirling a blue-and-white scarf above his head.

The original picture bag for the 7-inch vinyl record released in 1972...

The song, a jaunty ditty penned by songwriters Daniel Boone and Rod McQueen and with backing music provided by the Larry Page Orchestra, was released to mark Chelsea's achievement in reaching the 1972 League Cup final. At the time football records were still something of a novelty, but the commercial opportunities represented by linking up a popular team with a decent tune were already apparent. In 1970, for instance, the England World Cup squad had topped the charts with *Back Home* before flying off to Mexico to defend the Jules Rimet trophy. Then, a year later, Arsenal reached Number 16 with their FA Cup final record, *Good*

Blue Is The Colour
THE CHELSEA FOOTBALL TEAM

BLUE IS THE COLOUR

Old Arsenal, a rather dreary effort set to the tune of *Rule Britannia* and with lyrics by long-chinned football pundit Jimmy Hill. With a livelier, more catchy song to work with there was every reason to believe that the Blues would get higher in the charts than the Gunners, but much would depend on the performance of the players when they put it down on vinyl.

On a cold February morning the whole Chelsea squad turned up at the Wessex Sound Studios, a converted church hall in Highbury, to record the song. Spotted by some young Gooners in the playground of the primary school opposite, the players were subjected to noisy chants of "What a load of rubbish!" as they were interviewed by a blonde female TV reporter outside the entrance to the studios. Most confessed to being nervous, although star striker Peter Osgood was

… after the Chelsea squad had recorded the track at a studio in Highbury!

his usual relaxed self, telling the reporter, "It's something terrific to do".

Their nerves eased by a few drinks, the players soon knocked out the single and also recorded an album, which included Osgood singing a solo version of the Middle of the Road chart-topper *Chirpy Chirpy Cheep Cheep*. Perhaps unsurprisingly, the album sank without trace but *Blue is the Colour* performed much better, reaching number five in the singles chart in March 1972 alongside classics such as T Rex's *Telegram Sam* and Nilsson's *Without You*.

During the song's climb up the charts the Blues were asked to appear on *Top of the Pops* at the BBC Television Centre at White City, an event that has gone down in Chelsea legend. Unimpressed by the players' fashionable leather jackets and flared trousers, the show's producer sent out a minion to buy 16 identical jumpers from Marks and Spencer so that the team would look "like a proper group". A more pressing concern was that the squad would be singing the song live – a daunting challenge for some professional groups let alone a bunch of amateurs. "We made an awful racket, just terrible," recalled midfielder John Boyle of the rehearsals. Once again, though, the players' vocal chords were

Dance troupe Pan's People partied with the squad after an appearance on TV

lubricated by copious amounts of alcohol to great effect. "We went back on stage quite a bit later," said 'Boylers', "and suddenly it was like having 16 Frank Sinatras!"

Watching the programme on TV, some eagle-eyed Chelsea fans might have noticed an unfamiliar face alongside Ossie and co. "There was a fan with us, a friend of Ian Hutchinson, and for a laugh we sneaked him into the group at the back," recalled defender John Dempsey. "People watching at home must have wondered who he was." To cap a great day, many of the players made a beeline for one of their favourite King's Road haunts afterwards, along with the girls from the show's in-house dance group, Pan's People.

Blue is the Colour stayed in the charts for 12 weeks, its popularity seemingly unaffected by Chelsea's surprise defeat by Stoke City at Wembley. In the years since it has seen off a few challengers, notably Suggs's 1997 FA Cup final offering *Blue Day*, to remain the song most closely associated with the club, while also inspiring numerous cover versions around the sporting world. True, it may not have topped the charts like *Back Home* and a later England World Cup release, *World in Motion*, but for most Chelsea fans *Blue is the Colour* has no rival as the all-time number one football song.

CHELSEA
COMIC STRIP HISTORY
2

IN OCTOBER 1932, CHELSEA'S MATCH AT BLACKPOOL WENT AHEAD DESPITE A FREEZING COLD WIND AND SUB-ZERO TEMPERATURES...

IN THE SECOND HALF, FOUR CHELSEA PLAYERS DECIDED THEY'D HAD ENOUGH AND RUSHED OFF TO THE WARMTH OF THE DRESSING ROOM...

THE STURDY NORTHERNERS REMAINED AT FULL STRENGTH AND TOOK FULL ADVANTAGE, WINNING THE GAME 4-0...

STORY OF THE BLUES
A FIRST TITLE
1940-63

Despite the ever-present threat of bombing raids by the Luftwaffe, football continued at Stamford Bridge during the Second World War, albeit on a regional basis. With clubs allowed to field as many 'guest' players as they wanted, new Chelsea boss Billy Birrell, formerly QPR manager, was able to call on the services of any big name who happened to be passing through London.

Among the array of stars who turned out for the club were Matt Busby, Arsenal legend Eddie Hapgood and future England manager Walter Winterbottom. The war years also saw Chelsea play at Wembley for the first time, the Pensioners losing to Charlton in the Football League (South) Cup Final in 1944 before winning the same competition the following season.

When league football restarted in August 1946 Chelsea's team contained just one name, winger Dickie Spence, who had played in the last pre-war fixture. The rest of the side included a number of regular 'guests' who had been signed up on a permanent basis, notably skipper John Harris and, most excitingly, England centre forward Tommy Lawton, a record £11,500 recruit from Everton. After little more than a season, though, Lawton moved on to Notts County to be replaced by Newcastle's Roy Bentley. The comings-and-goings made little difference to the club's mediocre form, although a good FA Cup run in 1950 raised supporters' hopes until they were shattered by an unlucky defeat to Arsenal in the semi-final.

A year later Chelsea looked certain to be relegated when, with just four games to play, they were anchored to the foot of the table six points from safety. What followed was an escape act Harry Houdini would have been proud of, as Birrell's men defeated Liverpool, Wolves, Fulham and Bolton to end the season level on points with Sheffield Wednesday and Everton. The maths boffins were called in and, to much rejoicing in

Chelsea keeper Charlie Thomson gathers the ball at the Bridge v Newcastle in February 1955

Chelsea's first League title-winning side show off the trophy in 1955

west London, Chelsea were found to have the best goal average of the trio, and so survived the dreaded drop. After another narrow escape the following season (and another *Groundhog Day*-style FA Cup semi-final defeat by the Gunners), Birrell was replaced as manager by Ted Drake, a former England international striker and previously manager of Reading.

Drake quickly made his mark off the pitch, ditching the Chelsea Pensioner from the club badge and introducing a new nickname, 'The Blues'. His team, though, were once again embroiled in a relegation struggle, only securing safety with a 3–1 home win over Manchester City on the final day of the 1952/53 season. The squad clearly needed strengthening, and

The League
championship trophy
is paraded before the
Stamford Bridge crowd
on the opening day of
the 1955/56 season

Drake exploited his knowledge of the lower divisions
to recruit the likes of winger Frank Blunstone,
centre-half Stan Wicks and inside forwards Les Stubbs
and John McNichol from unfashionable clubs at
knockdown prices.

After an encouraging eighth place finish in 1954,
Drake's revamped team started the following season
with high expectations. However, after a run of
four consecutive defeats in October their campaign
appeared to be in tatters. This, though, was an

extremely open, unpredictable league and by the turn of the year Chelsea were one of eight clubs separated by just two points at the top of the table. As their rivals continued to take points off each other, the Blues hit a run of consistent form at precisely the right time, replacing Wolves at the summit after a 1-0 win at Cardiff in March. When, on Easter Saturday, Chelsea beat Wolves by the same score in front of a huge crowd of over 75,000 at the Bridge the title was theirs for the taking. Two weeks later a comfortable 3-0 home win over already-relegated Sheffield Wednesday sealed the club's first ever championship, the Blues finishing four points clear of Wolves, Portsmouth and Sunderland. "I have all the honours first-class soccer has to offer – but this tops the lot of 'em," an emotional Drake told supporters after the match.

Inevitably perhaps, the rest of the 1950s were something of an anti-climax. The championship side was a relatively old one and was soon broken up. In its place came a group of young players, dubbed 'Drake's Ducklings', who proved to be frustratingly inconsistent. They did, though, include one genuine superstar in the form of Jimmy Greaves, a prolific teenage striker who scored on his debut at Tottenham in 1957 and banged in another 131 goals in just four seasons before he was lured overseas by AC Milan.

Greaves was still at the club when the Blues made their European debut, getting through to the second round of the Inter-Cities Fairs Cup in 1959 before losing to Red Star Belgrade. The following season a clutch of young players, including goalkeeper Peter Bonetti, striker Bobby Tambling and midfielder Terry Venables, all gained valuable first-team experience in the same year that they won the FA Youth Cup.

However, the departure of the talismanic Greaves hit Chelsea hard, and in 1962 the Blues were relegated to the Second Division after a 32-year stay in the top

flight. The club's poor form spelt the end for Drake, who was replaced as manager by his young chief coach, wise-cracking Scot Tommy Docherty. 'The Doc' set about building a new team, promoting youngsters like Ron 'Chopper' Harris, striker Barry Bridges and winger Bert Murray while unceremoniously booting out most of the old stagers.

A 17-year-old Jimmy Greaves runs rings around Spurs in August 1957

Playing a high tempo game orchestrated by the clever Venables, the Blues quickly surged to the top of the Second Division, leading the field by seven points at Christmas. Promotion seemed assured until the arrival of 'the Big Freeze', Arctic weather conditions gripping the whole of the country. In the first nine weeks of 1963 the Blues only played two League games, losing both to allow Sunderland to take over at the top. However, a 1-0 win at Roker Park in the penultimate game of the season put Chelsea ahead of the Wearsiders before a 7-0 demolition of Portsmouth at the Bridge secured second place behind champions Stoke.

The Blues were back where they belonged and one of the most exciting periods in Chelsea history was about to begin...

KIT PARADE

Shortly after joining Chelsea from Sampdoria
in 1995, Ruud Gullit revealed that the Blues' kit played
a small part in persuading him to leave Italy for west
London. "Chelsea play in white socks. I always win things
in white socks," the former World Player of the Year
told reporters at his unveiling, perhaps unaware that
the Blues had only recently re-adopted his favourite line
in footwear after sporting blue socks during the late
1980s and early 1990s.

The club's kit history, though, shows that it is
not just Chelsea's socks which have changed
and developed over the years – the shirts and
shorts, too, have altered quite radically
since the Londoners started out in
1905. Initially, Chelsea wore
light blue shirts to match
the racing colours of the
club's first president, Earl
Cadogan, the new team's kit being
completed by white shorts and dark
blue socks. Two years later, in
February 1907, the club donned
shirts of a darker shade of blue for
the first time when Nottingham
Forest visited Stamford Bridge,
although this significant change was
not made official until 1912. For
many years afterwards Chelsea's kit
remained essentially unaltered

The trademark
dark Chelsea
blue was officially
adopted in 1912

apart from the socks, which appeared in a variety of styles in the following decades including blue-and-white hoops (in the mid-1930s), black with white tops (in the late 1940s) and black with red, white and blue tops (in the late 1950s).

The iconic, Cup-winning kit of the early 1970s, with distinctive yellow trim

The trendy boutiques of the King's Road were at the centre of the rapidly changing fashions of the 1960s so it was apt that the Blues' kit should undergo the biggest transformation yet in this decade, manager Tommy Docherty approving a new strip made up of blue shirts with a white round-neck collar, blue shorts and white socks at the start of the 1964/65 season. While Chelsea's kit could easily have been confused with that of Everton or Leicester City in the past, the striking new design was utterly distinctive, the snazzy, modern look perfectly complementing the fast, upbeat playing style of a young Blues side.

A redesign in the late 1960s resulted in the white trimmings disappearing from the team's shirts and the famous lion crest replacing the squiggly 'CFC' logo on the earlier kit. Sported by the likes of Peter Osgood, Charlie Cooke and Ron 'Chopper' Harris, the combination of navy blue shirts and shorts and white socks was instantly recognisable and swiftly became one of the game's most iconic kits. Occasionally, as in the victorious 1970 FA Cup Final replay against Leeds and the 1972 League Cup Final defeat to Stoke, yellow socks and short trimmings would replace the usual white ones so as not to clash with the opposition.

In the mid-1970s floppy white collars were added to the shirts while the diamond logo of kit designers Umbro appeared for the first time. The following decade, meanwhile, saw the Blues sport a couple of innovative figure-hugging designs from Le coq sportif. The first, in the early 1980s, featured white pinstripes and, controversially, red trimmings around the v-neck and sleeves. The second, which was worn by the Blues during their 1983/84 promotion season and was the first Chelsea shirt to sport a sponsor's logo, became popular with fans thanks to the team's success, but traditionalists were appalled by the narrow horizontal lines of red that broke up two slightly different shades of blue on the jerseys.

After the mercifully short-lived 'Chelsea Collection', a poorly-received experiment in in-house kit design, the Blues renewed their association with Umbro in 1987, who remained the club's kit suppliers until the current relationship with Adidas was established in 2006. Highlights of the Umbro years included the dark blue strip with white piping that the Blues wore during their first ever Champions League campaign in 1999/2000 and the 'centenary' kit of 2005/06 which featured gold trimmings, hinting at the club's elite status as Premiership champions. Fans, though, were much less keen on the Umbro home kit of 1997-99, some feeling that the blue shirts simply weren't dark enough while others bemoaned the superfluous large white panels under the arms.

Pat Nevin sporting the red-edged kit that outraged the purists

The club's latest kit has also proved controversial thanks to the red in the v-neck collar, a nod to the famous scarlet coats of the Chelsea Pensioners. Time will tell whether it proves popular with the fans.

Chelsea's change colours have traditionally been either yellow or white, although numerous away kits have broken with this convention. The first to do so was a red, white and green strip introduced in 1972 by then manager Dave Sexton, who was an admirer of the great Hungarian side of the 1950s which wore the same colours. But although the Blues may have looked like the Magical Magyars they didn't play like them, and were relegated a couple of years after adopting the kit.

Tangerine and graphite helped push shirt design to new levels

Red again featured prominently in Chelsea's away kit of the late 1980s, notably in the form of a red-and-white-hooped Rugby League-style shirt which the Blues wore during the 1989 Second Division championship-winning campaign, and a red-and-white chequered affair which appeared two seasons later.

By the mid-1990s the thriving market in replica shirts provided clubs with a valuable income stream which encouraged them to introduce new away kits regularly. At the same time, kit suppliers were given more freedom to experiment with the design of away shirts, as clubs attempted to outdo each other in the fashion stakes.

Chelsea's notorious 'tangerine and graphite' away kit of 1994-96 was one result of this design explosion, and it certainly drew a strong reaction from the fans: some loved it; many more thought it was completely hideous.

The Blues wore a black kit in 2002 – although, according to Umbro, the strip's actual colours were midnight blue and carbon. "We wanted something smart and sophisticated for a club that's traditionally been very stylish," revealed a spokesman for the company, neatly summing up the qualities many fans expect to see in a Chelsea kit. In the years since, black has been the pre-eminent colour in the club's away strips although Adidas bucked the trend in 2007 with a luminous yellow shirt which resembled a cyclist's safety garment.

No doubt, the kit designers will continue to come up with some startlingly innovative away kits. Most fans will happily accept that, although they won't appreciate too much meddling with the Blues' famous home strip...and that includes those traditional white socks which so impressed Ruud Gullit.

Florent Malouda in Chelsea's 2010/11 kit

HALL OF FAME

ROY BENTLEY

Top goalscorer in all of the eight seasons he played for the club, Roy Bentley wrote himself into the history books when he skippered the Blues to their first ever league title in 1955.

Bentley signed for Chelsea from Newcastle in January 1948, partially on the advice of his doctor who had suggested that a move south would improve the lung problems he occasionally suffered from. Previously Bentley had played for both Bristol clubs during the war, much of which he spent serving with the Royal Navy on board destroyers which escorted Atlantic convoys.

His early months at Stamford Bridge were far from happy. Struggling for form, he was compared unfavourably by fans to his predecessor at centre forward, Tommy Lawton, one of whom once advised him to "Get back to Newcastle where you belong." This incident proved to be a turning point. "I thought, 'You bastard. I'll show you,'" he later recalled. The next season Bentley silenced his critics by scoring 23 goals, while none of his team-mates made it into double figures.

A natural athlete who had excelled at the high jump, hurdling and sprinting at school, he possessed two good feet and was a powerful header of the ball. These attributes impressed the England selectors who called Bentley up for his international debut against Sweden in 1949. The following year he scored the winning goal against Scotland at Hampden Park which booked his country's passage to the 1950 World Cup in Brazil, a tournament in which he also figured.

His greatest achievement, though, came five years later when he led the Blues to an unexpected league title triumph. As ever, Bentley was the main focus of the attack, contributing 21 league goals, including a vital double in a thrilling 4-3 away win at closest challengers Wolves. The following season proved to be his last at the club as Bentley moved on to neighbours Fulham in the summer of 1956.

He later played for QPR and managed both Reading and Swansea City, leading the Welsh club to promotion to the old Third Division in 1970.

> **❝ Roy was a tremendous player, a great captain and, in many ways, he was like a father to us all in our title season ❞**
>
> 1950s Chelsea goalkeeper Chic Thomson

Born: Bristol, 17th May 1924
Chelsea appearances: 347
Chelsea goals: 150
Honours won with Chelsea: League title (1955)
Other clubs: Bristol City (1941-46), Newcastle United (1946-48), Fulham (1956-60), QPR (1960-62)
International appearances: England, 12 caps (1949-55)

ROY BENTLEY FACTFILE

PETER BONETTI

Considered by many to be Chelsea's greatest goalkeeper, Peter Bonetti was a fixture between the posts at the Bridge for two decades and a key member of the exciting Blues side that enjoyed cup success in the early 1970s.

Slim and only five feet ten inches, Bonetti did not look like a typical goalkeeper. However, he made up for his less than imposing physique with great athleticism, lightning reflexes and outstanding agility – a combination of qualities that earned him the nickname of 'The Cat'. Perhaps his only weakness was his kicking, his goal kicks often struggling to reach the halfway line.

Born in Putney to parents of Swiss origin, the young Bonetti got his break after his mother wrote a letter to Chelsea manager Ted Drake suggesting her son "might make you a useful goalkeeper".

After impressing at a trial and signing pro in April 1959, he made his debut the following year in a 3-0 home win against Manchester City and soon became first-choice number one at the expense of former England international Reg Matthews.

A League Cup winner in 1965, Bonetti was a central figure when Chelsea won the FA Cup for the first time in 1970. He performed heroically in the final against Leeds, pulling off a series of stunningly acrobatic saves at Wembley and then manfully carrying on in the replay at Old Trafford despite suffering a bad knee injury early on. The following year he was again in fine form as the Blues beat Real Madrid in Athens to win the European Cup Winners' Cup.

By 1975 Bonetti's long and distinguished Chelsea career appeared to be over when he was allowed to join American club St Louis Stars on a free transfer.

A goalkeeping crisis at the Bridge, though, led to his return and the grey-haired veteran served for another four years, a highlight of which was the promotion campaign of 1976/77.

A true Chelsea hero, Bonetti eventually retired in 1979 after clocking up 729 games for the Blues – a figure only surpassed by his equally legendary team-mate, Ron 'Chopper' Harris.

> **ff A fantastic athlete. Brave as a lion and an inspirational team-mate for any pro. He saved our bacon on many a day JJ**
> Chelsea team-mate Charlie Cooke

Born: Putney, 27th September 1941

Chelsea appearances: 729

Chelsea goals: 0

Honours won with Chelsea: League Cup (1965), FA Cup (1970), European Cup Winners' Cup (1971)

Other clubs: St Louis Stars (1975), Dundee United (1979)

International appearances: England, 7 caps (1966-70)

PETER BONETTI FACTFILE

KERRY DIXON

The second highest goalscorer in Chelsea history, Kerry Dixon joined Chelsea for a bargain £175,000 from Reading in the summer of 1983.

Powerful, quick, strong in the air and possessing a ferocious shot in both feet, the blonde-haired Dixon had all the qualities any manager could wish for in a centre forward, despite occasional doubts expressed about his first touch. He immediately formed a terrific striking partnership with the tigerish David Speedie as the Blues stormed back into the top flight in 1984 after a five-year absence. Dixon's 36 goals, which included a magnificent hat-trick in the promotion-clinching 5-0 demolition of old rivals Leeds at the Bridge, was the best tally by a Chelsea player for over two decades. Another excellent campaign at the higher level led to a first international call-up in 1985, Dixon scoring twice in a friendly against West Germany on his full England debut. In three consecutive seasons he had topped the scoring charts in the Third, Second and First Divisions but, after suffering a torn stomach muscle against Liverpool in 1986, his form dipped along with that of the Blues, who were relegated two years later.

A solitary season back in the Second Division in 1988/89 proved to be a welcome tonic, Dixon notching 25 league goals as he formed another prolific partnership, this time with Gordon Durie. The Shed idol hit another 20 the next season as the Blues celebrated their return to the big time by finishing fifth, their highest league position since 1970.

By the time he moved on to Southampton in the summer of 1992, he had scored an incredible 193 goals for Chelsea – nine short of Bobby Tambling's all-time club record. Indeed, but for a poor final season at the Bridge and a catalogue of missed penalties earlier in his Blues career, Dixon would surely have fulfilled his aim of setting a new club goalscoring benchmark. Nonetheless, despite the disappointment of falling short of his target, he had already done more than enough to secure his place in the Chelsea hall of fame.

> **❝ He made life easy for me. He just knew where to go. He had pace, power, and he must have been a dream for a manager ❞**
>
> 1980s team-mate Pat Nevin

Born: Luton, 24th July 1961
Chelsea appearances: 420
Chelsea goals: 193
Honours won with Chelsea: Second Division (1984, 1989)
Other clubs: Reading (1980-83), Southampton (1992-93), Luton Town (1993-95), Millwall (1995-96), Watford (1996), Doncaster Rovers (1996-97)
International appearances: England, 8 caps (1985-86)

KERRY DIXON FACTFILE

DIDIER DROGBA

A one-man forward line who can batter a defence into submission virtually on his own, Didier Drogba has been an instrumental figure in Chelsea's success since Roman Abramovich bought the club in 2003.

Signed the following year from Marseille for £24 million by long-time admirer Jose Mourinho, the Ivorian striker had a difficult start to his Stamford Bridge career. Despite helping the Blues win back-to-back Premiership titles, Drogba was dogged by accusations of diving and failed to show his best form consistently. It was a different story in 2006/07 when he claimed the Golden Boot after scoring 33 goals in all competitions, including match-winning goals in the Carling Cup and FA Cup finals.

His ability to decide the outcome of the biggest of occasions was again demonstrated in the following season, when two well-taken goals against Liverpool took the Blues through to their first ever Champions League final. Unfortunately, his suspect temperament let him down in Moscow, where he was sent off in extra-time for slapping Manchester United defender Nemanja Vidic. A year later, Drogba lost his head again in the same competition after Chelsea's controversial semi-final exit at the hands of Barcelona, confronting the Norwegian referee who had denied the Blues four clear penalties and swearing into a TV camera. Another European ban inevitably followed.

If he is feeling a good sensation about the game, if he is confident, he is impossible to play against

Chelsea manager Carlo Ancelotti

When Drogba manages to keep his passionate nature under control, though, there is no doubt that he is a phenomenal player. Strong, fast, capable of shooting powerfully with either foot and deadly in the air, he is a defender's nightmare brought to life. He is now 32 yet there are no signs that he is a force in decline and, indeed, the 2009/10 season was his best yet. An impressive total of 29 league goals saw him collect the Golden Boot for a second time, while a magnificent curled free-kick in the FA Cup final against Portsmouth sealed the Double in splendid style. It was the seventh goal Drogba had scored for the Blues in six domestic finals, a remarkable statistic that underlies his legendary status with the club's fans.

Born: Abidjan, Ivory Coast, 11th March 1978

Chelsea appearances: 260

Chelsea goals: 131

Honours won with Chelsea: Premiership (2005, 2006, 2010), FA Cup (2007, 2009, 2010), Carling Cup (2005, 2007)

Other clubs: Le Mans (1998-2002), En Avant Guingamp (2002-03), Marseille (2002-03)

International appearances: Ivory Coast, 70 (2002-)

DIDIER DROGBA FACTFILE

RON HARRIS

An uncompromising defender whose crunching tackles earned him the nickname 'Chopper', Ron Harris captained the entertaining Chelsea side of the late 1960s and early 1970s.

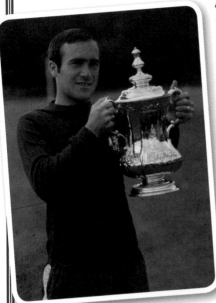

A talented all-round sportsman who was on the Lord's ground staff for a while, Harris followed in the footsteps of his older brother, Allan, joining Chelsea as a junior on £7.50 a week. He played in the side that won the FA Youth Cup in 1961 and the following year made his first-team debut, aged 17, in a home win against Sheffield Wednesday. He had to wait until the last month of the 1962/63 promotion season before establishing himself, and remained a fixture in the Chelsea team for the next 17 years.

In 1966 he was appointed captain by boss Tommy Docherty, succeeding Terry Venables. He led Chelsea in the club's first FA Cup final at Wembley against Spurs in 1967, but had to settle for a runners-up medal following a 2-1 defeat. Three years later he was back at the Twin Towers for the final against Leeds, a match he only managed to play in after having a pain-killing injection for a thigh injury. Typically, he still performed well although his major contribution to Chelsea's success came in the replay at Old Trafford when, switched from central defence to right-back, he neutralised Leeds's dangerous Scottish winger Eddie Gray. The following year Harris collected more silverware, this time the European Cup Winners' Cup after the Blues beat Real Madrid in Athens.

His image was as one of soccer's hard men, but Harris was a decent footballer who passed the ball intelligently and rarely gave away possession. Comfortable anywhere in defence he could also play in midfield – and did so for much of his final season at the Bridge in 1979/80. He was probably at his best when employed as a limpet-like man-marker against the opposition's most dangerous player.

By the time he joined Brentford as player/coach in 1980 he had set a new club appearance record of 795 games, a total which is unlikely ever to be beaten.

> **ff Ron was one of the greatest man-to-man markers in the world. No one ever got past him, he was tough and a superb tackler JJ**
> 1960s and 1970s team-mate Tommy Baldwin

Born: Hackney, London, 13th November 1944

Chelsea appearances: 795

Chelsea goals: 14

Honours won with Chelsea: League Cup (1965), FA Cup (1970), European Cup Winners' Cup (1971)

Other clubs: Brentford (1980-83), Aldershot (1984-85)

RON HARRIS FACTFILE

FRANK LAMPARD

The third highest scorer in Chelsea history, Frank Lampard has emerged as one of the best players in the world since joining the Blues from West Ham in an £11 million deal in 2001.

After a quiet start to his Chelsea career, Lampard quickly developed new facets to his game which made him much more than the industrious box-to-box player he had been as a youngster at Upton Park. His range of passing improved dramatically while his shooting from distance, cleverly-timed attacking runs and composed finishing inside the area brought him a seasonal goals tally most strikers would envy.

His first major honour arrived in the form of the Carling Cup in February 2005, swiftly followed by the Premiership title a couple of months later, Lampard clinching the trophy for the Blues with two trademark goals on a memorable afternoon at Bolton's Reebok Stadium.

The football writers promptly made Lampard their

Footballer of the Year, while in the same year he was runner-up to Ronaldinho in the European and World Footballer of the Year polls.

The Blues' vice-captain enjoyed another excellent season as the club retained the title in 2006, and the following year he was again instrumental as Chelsea claimed the domestic cup double, Lampard setting up Didier Drogba for the winning goal in the FA Cup final against Manchester United.

The same opponents gained revenge by winning the Champions League final in Moscow in 2008, although Lampard had the consolation of grabbing the Blues' goal before the match was settled by penalties. Weeks earlier in the semi-final against Liverpool he had demonstrated his calm assurance and professionalism by coolly scoring from the spot just days after the death of his mother from pneumonia.

The following year he scored the winner in the FA Cup final against Everton, before enjoying his best ever season in 2009/10. Inevitably, Lampard was a key figure as the Blues won their first league and cup Double, the midfielder contributing 27 goals in all competitions to cement his place as one of Chelsea's all-time greats.

> **For me he is the best player in the world. I would not change Lampard for another player because he does everything**
>
> Former Chelsea manager
> Jose Mourinho

Born: **Romford**, 20th June 1978
Chelsea appearances: 477
Chelsea goals: 157
Honours won with Chelsea:
Premiership (2005, 2006, 2010), **Carling Cup** (2005, 2007),
FA Cup (2007, 2009, 2010)
Other clubs: **Swansea City** (1995-96, loan), **West Ham United** (1996-2002)
International appearances: **England**, 78 caps (1999-)

FRANK LAMPARD FACTFILE

PETER OSGOOD

Dubbed 'The King of Stamford Bridge' by the legions of Blues fans who idolised him, Peter Osgood was the greatest individual talent in the flamboyant Chelsea side of the late 1960s and early 1970s.

A tall, elegant striker with a wonderfully deft touch, a good turn of pace and the ability to shoot with both feet, Osgood burst onto the Bridge scene as a 17-year-old, scoring twice on his debut in a League Cup tie against Workington in December 1964. The following season he became a regular in Tommy Docherty's young Blues side, his outstanding performances in both the domestic and European arena earning him a place in England manager Alf Ramsay's initial squad of 40 for the 1966 World Cup.

A broken leg, sustained later that year in a match against Blackpool, halted his progress for a while but in 1970 he was a central figure as the Blues won the FA Cup, scoring in every round of the competition including, most memorably, a brilliant diving header at Old Trafford in the cup final replay against arch rivals Leeds. The following season another superb strike helped the Blues win the European Cup Winners' Cup against Real Madrid in Athens. Always the man for the big occasion, Osgood also netted in the 1972 League Cup final against Stoke, although his goal couldn't prevent the Blues going down to a surprise defeat.

In March 1974 Osgood was sold to Southampton for a club record £275,000, Chelsea boss Dave Sexton having tired of his star striker's sometimes casual attitude in training and keen membership of the Bridge drinking club. Four years later, and clearly past his best, he briefly returned to help the cash-strapped Blues in an ultimately fruitless battle against relegation before retiring in 1979.

Following his sudden death from a heart attack in March 2006, Ossie's ashes were buried beneath the penalty spot at the Shed End. Gone but most certainly not forgotten, his memory lives on at the Bridge – most poignantly in the 'Osgood' song which can often be heard at home games.

> **Ossie had everything. He was as good in the air as he was on the ball. He was a joy to play with and he both scored and made a hell of a lot of goals**
>
> Strike partner Ian Hutchinson

PETER OSGOOD FACTFILE

Born: Windsor, 20th February 1947

Died: 1st March 2006

Chelsea appearances: 380

Chelsea goals: 150

Honours won with Chelsea: FA Cup (1970), European Cup Winners' Cup (1971)

Other clubs: Southampton (1974-77), Norwich City (1976-77, loan), Philadelphia Fury (1978)

International appearances: England, 4 caps (1970-73)

JOHN TERRY

The most successful captain in Chelsea's history, John Terry has been a rock-like presence at the heart of the Blues' defence for a decade.

A Chelsea youth product who started out as a ball-playing midfielder, Terry made his first-team debut as a substitute against Aston Villa in October 1998. After a brief spell on loan at Nottingham Forest he established himself in the Blues' side in the 2000/01 campaign, his ultra-committed performances earning him the Chelsea Player of the Year award.

His progress was such that he was soon filling in as the team's skipper in the absence of Marcel Desailly, taking the role on a permanent basis when new manager Jose Mourinho arrived at the Bridge in the summer of 2004. Terry went on to enjoy an outstanding season, leading the Blues to the Premiership title and picking up the PFA Player of the Year award. When

Chelsea retained the Premiership title in 2006 he was an equally important figure, again earning plaudits for his excellent reading of the game and intelligent distribution from the back as well as for his more obvious defensive attributes.

The following year saw Terry collect more winners' medals in both the Carling Cup and the FA Cup, the Chelsea skipper returning from hospital to join in the celebrations for the first of those triumphs after being knocked unconscious following a typically brave challenge in a crowded penalty area. A far more painful blow for Terry, though, was the penalty miss in the 2008 Champions League final shoot-out which cost the Blues the chance to claim the biggest prize of all. Unfortunate it may have been, but the episode again illustrated Terry's willingness to take on a weighty responsibility which others were only too keen to avoid.

Despite losing the England captaincy in February 2010 following newspaper allegations about his private life, Terry skippered the Blues to the Double by the end of the season, his qualities as a leader undiminished by the controversy that surrounded him.

> **ff I have been all over the world and I have never seen a captain like him JJ**
> Former Chelsea manager
> Avram Grant

JOHN TERRY FACTFILE

Born: Barking, 7th December 1980

Chelsea appearances: 458
Chelsea goals: 38
Honours won with Chelsea: Premiership (2005, 2006, 2010),
FA Cup (2000, 2007, 2009, 2010), Carling Cup (2005, 2007)

Other clubs: Nottingham Forest (2000, loan)

International appearances: England, 60 (2003-)

DENNIS WISE

A combative midfielder with the Blues for over a decade, Dennis Wise was a huge crowd favourite who skippered Chelsea to cup glory five times between 1997 and 2000.

Wise joined Chelsea in the summer of 1990 for a then club record £1.6 million from Wimbledon, with whom he had won the FA Cup two years earlier. His career at the Bridge got off to a less than auspicious start when he was sent off for fighting with Crystal Palace's Andy Gray in his second match for his new club. By the end of the season, though, he had impressed sufficiently to earn his first England cap, marking his international debut by scoring the winner away to Turkey.

He was appointed captain by new manager Glenn Hoddle at the start of the 1993/94 season and at the end of the campaign lead out the Blues in the FA Cup final. There was to be no happy ending, though, as Manchester United cruised to a 4-0 victory.

Despite the arrival of big-name foreign signings at the Bridge from the mid-1990s onwards, Wise remained the linchpin of the Blues' side, his tireless running, committed tackling and incisive passing all vital elements in the team's chemistry. The second half of his Chelsea career saw Wise collect a haul of silverware that could have filled Aladdin's cave: two FA Cups, the European Cup Winners' Cup, the European Super Cup and the Coca-Cola Cup. Perhaps, too, he might have lifted the Premiership trophy in 1999 had he not been suspended for 15 games that season – his punishment for a number of red cards during that campaign. following season, though, Wise put in some superb performances in the Champions League, notably away to AC Milan where he scored a memorable goal in the San Siro which is still recalled in song by the Chelsea faithful.

"His personality makes the difference. You can have all the skill and ability but it is personality on the field which gives you status"
Chelsea boss Gianluca Vialli, 2000

Twice voted Chelsea Player of the Year (in 1998 and 2000) Wise moved on to Leicester City in June 2001 after making 445 appearances for the Blues, a total surpassed by just five other players.

Born: Kensington, 16th December 1966
Chelsea appearances: 445
Chelsea goals: 76
Honours won with Chelsea: FA Cup (1997, 2000), European Cup Winners' Cup (1998), Coca-Cola Cup (1998), European Super Cup (1998)
Other clubs: Wimbledon (1985-90), Leicester City (2001-02), Millwall (2002-05), Southampton (2005-06), Coventry City (2006)
International appearances: England, 21 caps (1991-2000)

DENNIS WISE FACTFILE

GIANFRANCO ZOLA

Few, if any, overseas players have made as big an impact in the Premiership as Gianfranco Zola, who joined Chelsea from Parma in November 1996 for £4.5 million.

In his first season at the Bridge the pint-sized Italian formed a tremendous attacking partnership with Mark Hughes as the Blues won the FA Cup, their first major trophy for 26 years. Zola, whose dazzling ball control, powerful shooting and visionary passing had earned rave reviews throughout the campaign, was named Footballer of the Year at the end of the season, the first Chelsea player ever to win this coveted award. He was a pivotal figure again the following year, helping the Blues win the Coca-Cola Cup and then coming off the bench to score a sensational winner against Stuttgart in the European Cup Winners' Cup final in Stockholm. Incredibly, when he smashed a rising shot into the top corner of the net from the edge of the box, he had only been on the pitch for 21 seconds.

He collected another FA Cup winners' medal in 2000, providing the chance for fellow Italian international Roberto di Matteo to score the only goal of the match after Aston Villa goalkeeper David James failed to hold onto his dipping, swerving free-kick. Although not always a regular starter in his latter years at the club, Zola continued to conjure up some memorable moments for his adoring public, none more special than an extraordinary backheel volley goal against Norwich in 2002. The following season proved to be his last at the Bridge, but he went out in some style by winning the club's Player of the Year trophy for a second time.

In the summer of 2003 Zola joined Cagliari in his native Sardinia, and in the same year was voted Chelsea's greatest ever player by the club's fans. A genuine Blues legend, Zola's name is sung at every Chelsea match, his popularity unaffected even by his surprise appointment as manager of London rivals West Ham in September 2008.

> **Everywhere we went we made friends because of him and I think he has been the most popular Italian in England**
>
> Former Chelsea manager Claudio Ranieri

Born: Oliena, Sardinia, 5th July 1966

Chelsea appearances: 312

Chelsea goals: 80

Honours won with Chelsea: FA Cup (1997, 2000), European Cup Winners' Cup (1998), Coca-Cola Cup (1998), European Super Cup (1998)

Other clubs: Nuorese (1984-87), Torres (1987-89), Napoli (1989-93), Parma (1993-96), Cagliari (2003-05)

International appearances: Italy, 35 caps (1991-97)

GIANFRANCO ZOLA FACTFILE

THE YOUNG ONES

In the same month that Chelsea clinched a first ever league and cup Double, the club won another prestigious trophy: the FA Youth Cup. Admittedly, the youngsters' triumph was not greeted with quite the same fanfare as the first team's successes, but nonetheless there was a healthy crowd of around 12,000 at Stamford Bridge to see the Blues' youth team come from behind to beat Aston Villa 2-1 on the night and 3-2 on aggregate. The victory was especially sweet as it was the club's first in the competition for nearly half a century, since a side containing the likes of Ron Harris, Terry Venables and Bert Murray retained the trophy after beating Everton in the 1961 final.

However, it still remains to be seen whether the current crop of youth team players follow in the footsteps of those legendary names by becoming first-team regulars. Certainly, recent history suggests they may struggle to do so. Apart from the very obvious exception of John Terry, the club's homegrown players have found making the leap from the juniors to the seniors an extremely difficult challenge. In the Premier League era only a handful of players have bucked

Michael Duberry and Jody Morris in the mid-1990s and Robert Huth and Carlton Cole in the early 2000s. But even this quartet found their first-team opportunities at Stamford Bridge limited and eventually moved on.

Given that the stated aim of the Chelsea Academy is "to produce homegrown professional footballers capable of competing with Europe's elite players" it's not hard to see why so many youngsters who start out with the club never get within sniffing distance of first-team action – the required standard is simply too high. In past seasons that didn't matter too much as, bankrolled by Roman Abramovich's millions, the club could recruit top-of-the-range players from around Europe. That policy helped bring the Blues much success but did little for the prospects of young players coming through the ranks.

Captain Conor Clifford holds the Youth Cup aloft

That, though, may be about to change because of new rules introduced by the Premier League and UEFA. From the start of the 2010/11 season Premier League clubs must name at least eight players in a 25-man squad who have been trained for three years under the

age of 21 by a club in the English and Welsh professional system. "This will mean you just can't buy a team from abroad," explained Premier League chief executive Richard Scudamore when the new rule was announced. "We think it will give clubs an extra incentive to invest in youth."

Youth captain Conor Clifford in U17 action for the Republic of Ireland against Germany

UEFA, too, are doing their bit to encourage clubs to promote from within rather than shelling out huge sums on transfers. In an attempt to end what UEFA President Michel Platini describes as 'financial doping' the organisation will require that clubs qualifying for European competitions must break even and not make persistent losses by the start of the 2012/13 season. Clubs who have spent the most on wages and transfers, like Chelsea, will be the hardest hit by the new rule, and will have to try to develop more homegrown players as a result.

It is, then, perhaps fortunate that the Chelsea Academy appears to be in robust health at the present moment. "Our Academy is working very well to grow young players and the victory in the Youth Cup was very good", Blues boss Carlo Ancelotti said in May 2010.

"I think we have fantastic players with fantastic talents, but we have to wait and maintain them in the Academy because they are very young." Chelsea chairman Bruce Buck has also indicated that the 2010/11 season could see a number of young players gain similar experience as Jeffrey Bruma, Gael Kakuta, Fabio Borini and Patrick van Aanholt, four teenagers who all made first-team appearances during the Double-winning campaign.

So, who are the youngsters who are most likely to line up alongside John Terry and co. at some point in the near future? Three players from the FA Youth Cup-winning side stand out:

Jacopo Sala, an Italian Under-19 international who can play in a variety of positions on the right; Conor Clifford, an Irish Under-21 international central midfielder who scored the winner against Villa with a stunning 25-yard strike; and Josh McEachran, a highly-rated creative midfielder who has been with Chelsea since the age of eight and was captain of the England Under-16 side before stepping up to the Under-17s.

With talented performers like this trio coming off the production line, the huge investment in Chelsea's Academy at last appears to be paying off.

Chelsea's Josh McEachran and Nathaniel Chalobah were in the England team that won the 2010 U17 European Championship

STORY OF THE BLUES
RISE AND FALL
1964-91

With the fashionable King's Road on their doorstep, Chelsea's players found themselves at the epicentre of the Swinging Sixties and, by happy coincidence, the Blues had a team which was very much in sync with the mood of the time. Youthful, sharp and confident, the side created by manager Tommy Docherty was far from overawed at the prospect of mixing it with the powers of the day and after a season of consolidation in the First Division launched an audacious bid for the domestic treble in 1964/65...

In the end the Blues, now featuring names such as Peter Bonetti, Ron Harris, John Hollins and Peter Houseman who would become synonymous with the club as the decade progressed, had to settle for the League Cup after beating Leicester City in a two-legged final. The following season was another exciting one as the Blues saw off Italian giants Roma and AC Milan before falling to Barcelona in the semi-finals of the Fairs Cup, young striker Peter Osgood earning rave reviews for his performances during the campaign. Less positively, a surprise FA Cup semi-final defeat by Sheffield Wednesday led Docherty to take an axe to his team, Terry Venables, Barry Bridges and Bert Murray all departing, with skilful Scottish winger Charlie Cooke and bustling striker Tommy Baldwin filling their places.

In 1967 Chelsea finally reached Wembley, but went down limply to London rivals Tottenham in the FA Cup final. A few months later Docherty was gone after falling out with the board, replaced by his onetime coach, the cerebral Dave Sexton. Under the new man Chelsea continued to play bright, attacking football, with teenage prodigy Alan Hudson emerging as a true heir to Venables in midfield, but silverware remained elusive until the Blues won the FA Cup in

(From left) Ron Harris, George Graham, Terry Venables, John Hollins and Eddie McCreadie turn on the style

1970. The final against Leeds was an epic extending over 240 drama-filled minutes, a 2-2 draw at a mud-clogged Wembley being followed by a replay at Old Trafford which was decided by David Webb's header in extra-time. The next day thousands of jubilant fans lined the streets around Stamford Bridge as the Blues paraded the cup for the first time – an occasion none

of those present will ever forget.

The next season Chelsea cemented their reputation as cup kings by seeing off Real Madrid in the final of the European Cup Winners' Cup, defender John Dempsey and Osgood scoring the goals in a 2-1 victory in Athens. A third cup in three years appeared likely after the Blues reached the 1972 League Cup Final but they surprisingly went down to underdogs Stoke City. That defeat marked the end of the glory years. In 1974 star players Osgood and Hudson were sold for a combined fee in excess of half a million pounds, soon to be followed out of the Stamford Bridge exit by Sexton. Shorn of their best players and crippled with debts caused by the soaring costs involved in the building of the new East stand, the Blues fell into the Second Division the following year.

Now managed by Eddie McCreadie, a stalwart of the cup-winning era, and captained by 20-year-old midfielder Ray Wilkins, a young Chelsea side stormed back into the First Division two years later. McCreadie, though, sensationally left the club after a contract dispute that summer and the Blues' return to

Crowds jammed the streets of Chelsea to see Ron Harris and Peter Bonetti show off the FA Cup in 1970

The Cup Winners' Cup is tantalisingly close as Chelsea take to the pitch in Athens in 1971, but they would need a replay to lift the trophy

the top flight proved to be short-lived, a dismal season in 1978/79 culminating with relegation confirmed a full month before the end of the campaign.

Following the resignation of former Tottenham Double-winning captain Danny Blanchflower, the manager's position was filled by England's 1966 World Cup hat-trick hero Geoff Hurst. The Blues narrowly missed out on promotion in 1980 but, after a demoralised team failed even to score a single goal in the last two months of the following season, Hurst was unceremoniously sacked. The man who gave him his marching orders, longserving chairman Brian Mears, was soon clearing his desk as well and in 1982 Chelsea acquired a new owner, businessman Ken Bates handing over a single pound note to take control of a club saddled with huge debts and a decidedly second-rate team.

The only way, surely, was up. Or was it? The 1982/83 season was the worst in the club's history, a run of dreadful results in the second half of the campaign sending the Blues sliding towards the trapdoor to the Third Division. Disaster was averted, however, in the penultimate match at fellow strugglers Bolton when winger Clive Walker scored

the only goal of the game in the final minutes.

The next few months were busy ones for manager
John Neal, who raided the lower divisions to bring
in half a dozen promising young players, including
Reading striker Kerry Dixon, Clyde winger Pat
Nevin and Wrexham goalkeeper Eddie Niedzwiecki.

The new signings gelled immediately with the likes of energetic midfielder John Bumstead and skipper Colin Pates to form an exciting new team which cruised to promotion, pipping Sheffield Wednesday to the Second Division title with a final day victory at Grimsby.

Coach John Hollins succeeded Neal as Chelsea adapted well to life in the top flight, with two consecutive sixth place finishes. Soon though, disagreements behind the scenes led to the departure of influential players, including Dixon's feisty strike partner David Speedie, and an appalling sequence of results led to the Blues falling into the relegation play-off place in 1988. Their opponents in the final were Second Division Middlesbrough, who had the advantage of good form going into the death-or-glory encounter. Boro won 2-1 on aggregate and Chelsea were down.

Bolstered by two experienced players in Graham Roberts and Peter Nicholas and well led by manager Bobby Campbell, the Blues easily claimed the Second Division title the following season, racking up an impressive 99 points. Back in the First Division, with former Sunderland player Ian Porterfield soon taking over at the helm, the Londoners pottered along quite comfortably without seriously challenging the so-called 'Big Five' clubs, the prime forces behind the new Premier League which kicked off in 1992. Still, at least Chelsea were there – something that would have seemed highly unlikely just a decade earlier.

Goal machine Kerry Dixon celebrates another strike in 1985

CHELSEA
COMIC STRIP HISTORY
3

IN THEIR MATCH AGAINST IPSWICH IN 1970 CHELSEA SCORED THE GOAL THAT NEVER WAS...

MIDFIELDER ALAN HUDSON FIRED IN A SHOT WHICH HIT THE OUTSIDE OF THE GOAL STANCHION...

TO THE SURPRISE OF EVERYONE AND DESPITE THE PROTESTS OF THE IPSWICH PLAYERS, THE REFEREE AWARDED A GOAL!

IT NEVER WENT IN, REF!

CHELSEA WON THE GAME 2-1, LEAVING IPSWICH BOSS BOBBY ROBSON SEETHING AND PLEADING IN VAIN FOR A RE-MATCH...

ROBBED...

TACTICS

THE DOC'S OVERLAPPING FULL BACKS

A feature of the Blues' attacking play during the mid-1960s were the overlapping runs made by their full backs, youth product Ken Shellito and Eddie McCreadie, a bargain £5,000 signing from East Stirling. In urging the duo to get forward as often as possible Chelsea boss Tommy Docherty was influenced by the great Brazil side of the time, which had won the World Cup in both 1958 and 1962 with a pair of full backs, Djalma Santos and Nilton Santos, who combined their defensive duties with speedy forays deep into the opponents' half.

As quick as whippets, comfortable in possession and accurate crossers of the ball, both McCreadie and Shellito were ideally suited to their role as auxiliary wingers. Feeding on the clever passes of midfield playmaker Terry Venables and combining well with widemen Frank Blunstone and Bert Murray, the pair raced into advanced positions countless times over the course of the average 90 minutes, adding an extra dimension to the Blues' offensive play. "Tactically, we aim at the man over in attack," Docherty explained. "It is a kind of concertina movement. Running off the ball, and playing the ball off quickly, are the basic things for us."

Chelsea's innovative style of play earned the club many admirers, including West Germany manager Helmut Schoen. "You play like a South American team," he told Docherty. "Your full backs come like wingers. We haven't seen this before in Europe." Schoen was so impressed he invited Chelsea to play the West German national team in a friendly as part of their preparations for the 1966 World Cup, the Blues winning 1-0 in Duisberg in February 1965.

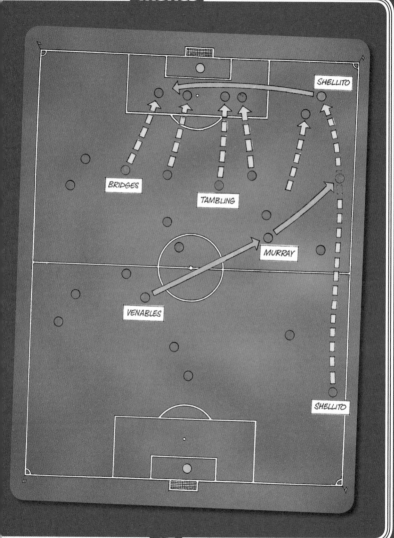

DIAMOND GEEZERS

In 1977 a young Chelsea side managed by former Blues defender Eddie McCreadie won promotion to the First Division in exciting style after enduring a two-year absence from the top flight of English football.

With no money available for transfers McCreadie's team largely consisted of home-grown youngsters who played with a verve and enthusiasm which struck a chord with their huge army of equally youthful fans. Tactically, McCreadie opted for a bold midfield diamond system which was designed to make the most of the attacking talents of Ray Wilkins, the Blues' 20-year-old captain and inspiration. Supported by tenacious tackler Ray Lewington at the base of the diamond and hard-working duo Garry Stanley and Ian Britton in the middle, Wilkins took up an advanced midfield role behind the strikers where he was well-placed to make a killer pass or fire off one of his trademark long-range shots. The England international positively thrived in the position, scoring nine goals during the campaign and laying on many others.

"A midfield diamond was quite unusual then, so Eddie was a bit ahead of his time," Wilkins later recalled. "He got me playing just behind the front two – Jock Finnieston and Kenny Swain – and it posed a problem for the opposition. They didn't know whether the defensive midfielder or the centre half should pick me up and I was getting into areas where I could do some damage with the great balls I was getting from the other guys. It was a creative and aggressive system and we put teams under a lot of pressure."

And, as the league table showed at the end of the season, the formation worked a treat.

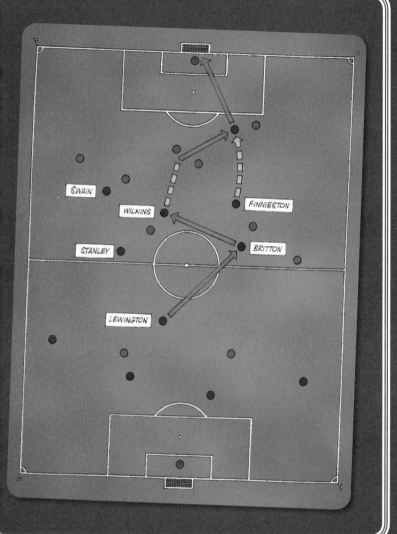

HODDLE'S SWEEPER SYSTEM

In the summer of 1993 Glenn Hoddle became Chelsea player/manager just a few weeks after leading Swindon into the Premiership.

Swindon's success owed much to the team's innovative 3-5-2 formation, with Hoddle himself directing operations from the back in the role of sweeper. In his first season at Chelsea, Hoddle adopted the same system, again filling the pivotal sweeper's position himself. However, his new charges struggled to adapt to the formation and it was swiftly abandoned after the Blues found themselves in the relegation zone at Christmas.

Two years later, though, the signing of former World Player of the Year Ruud Gullit gave Hoddle the opportunity to return to his preferred system. Although known primarily as a striker with AC Milan and Sampdoria, Gullit had started out as a sweeper with HFC Haarlem in his native Holland and was keen to reprise the role. What's more, he was more naturally suited to the position than Hoddle, possessing the strength and physical presence to deal with the defensive aspects of the role, as well as the skill, vision and pace to launch counter-attacks from deep.

"I hope you have all seen why the best position for Ruud is sweeper," Hoddle told the club newspaper *Onside*, while bemoaning media criticism that Gullit did not sprint back into defence after his forward forays. "It's there for everyone to see," he said, "the deep midfielder drops back into his position. He doesn't have to race back. That would be a waste of energy."

The best answer to the critics, though, came from Gullit himself when, in a home game against Southampton, he sauntered forward from the back before scoring with a glorious 20-yard volley.

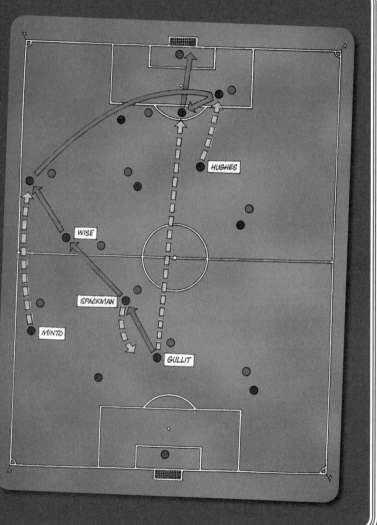

MOURINHO'S 4-3-3 SYSTEM

In the summer of 2004 Jose Mourinho arrived at Stamford Bridge from Porto, who he had just led to victory in the Champions League. Porto had triumphed in the final against Monaco employing a 4-3-1-2 system, with three defensive midfielders providing a solid base for Deco in the hole. Tweaking this formation slightly, Mourinho began the Premiership season with a diamond midfield but soon switched to a 4-3-3 line up with skilful wide players Damien Duff and Arjen Robben supporting lone striker Didier Drogba.

"Against a big team like us, the tendency is for our opponents to close us down," he explained, "so we must open things up. Width is important in a team like ours, and with the quality of our wingers we have to use them."

The system became Chelsea's trademark as the Blues won back-to-back Premiership titles in 2005 and 2006. As well as providing a threat down both flanks and through the middle, the formation ideally suited the attacking instincts of midfielder Frank Lampard, who frequently broke forward in support of the powerful Drogba into positions in and around the penalty area where he could test the goalkeeper. Meanwhile, midfield anchorman Claude Makelele would patrol the area in front of Chelsea's back four, looking to stifle any counter-attack by the opposition at the first opportunity.

Mourinho's system was so successful it was widely copied by other Premiership managers. However, lacking the creative talent available to the Blues' supremo, they tended to put the accent on defence, instructing their wide players to play deeper with the result that Chelsea's attack-minded 4-3-3 essentially became a dull, safety first 4-5-1.

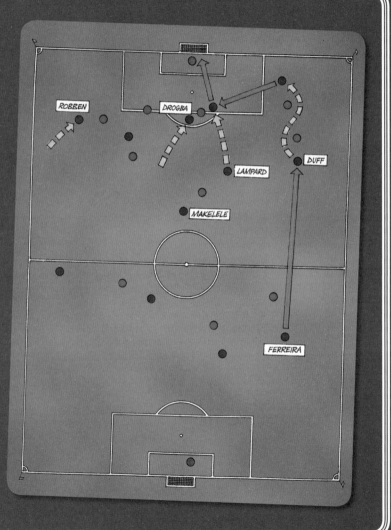

GREAT
GAFFERS

Now sometimes referred to as 'the impossible job', the role of Chelsea manager has always been a demanding one. Disappointingly, the majority of the Blues' bosses have failed to meet the challenge and, like Avram Grant and Luiz Felipe Scolari to name but two recent examples, have soon been pointed towards the Stamford Bridge exit.

A select band of managers have delivered success but, generally speaking, even they have found that depositing silverware in the club's trophy room was no guarantee of long-term job security.

Just ask Jose Mourinho. Hailed by supporters and press alike as a managerial genius after leading the Blues to two Premiership titles, the FA Cup and a pair of Carling Cups in just three

Jose Mourinho:
A bit special

glory-filled seasons, the
self-styled 'Special One'
might have thought he was
bullet-proof. Far from it. In
September 2007 he left the
club 'by mutual consent' after
falling out with Roman
Abramovich, Chelsea's
billionare owner. Mourinho's
demise was mourned not just
by Blues fans but the wider
football world, which had
warmed to his engagingly
charismatic personality,
headline-grabbing quips and
film-star good looks. Indeed,
at the height of Mourinho-
mania the maverick
Portuguese boss wasn't
just a regular on the sports
pages but on the news and
fashion pages, where he was

Gianluca Vialli moved
successfully from
pitch to dugout

lauded for his chic continental dress sense, a grey
wool Armani coat being a particular favourite of the
style commentators.

Chelsea's second most successful manager, Gianluca
Vialli, was also something of a fashion icon during his
stint at the Bridge in the late 1990s. Another devotee
of signor Armani, Vialli sported a highly fashionable
goatee beard which he liked to stroke while pondering

journalists' questions in press conferences. Often these were rather jingoistic enquiries about the lack of Englishmen in Vialli's side but, ever the gentleman, the Italian would politely reply that he would love to play more homegrown players provided they were better than the likes of Gianfranco Zola, Roberto di Matteo or Marcel Desailly. Few Chelsea fans cared about the dearth of British bulldogs in their cosmopolitan side, which won three major cups and two minor ones under Vialli in entertaining fashion before chairman Ken Bates gave the former Blues striker his P45 in September 2000.

Ruud Gullit with the 1997 FA Cup, won with his trademark 'sexy football'

Vialli's predecessor, dreadlocked Dutchman Ruud Gullit, was yet another Chelsea manager who was, in many ways, a bigger star than any of his players. A former World Player of the Year, Gullit was a sensation at the Bridge after being persuaded to sign for the Blues from Sampdoria in 1995 by then boss Glenn Hoddle. The following year he took over as player/manager, fulfilling his promise of providing 'sexy football' as his attack-minded side won the FA Cup in exciting style. A flamboyant figure, Gullit seemed the ideal Chelsea boss until, in February 1998 with the

Blues lying second in the
Premiership table, he was
sacked after making what the
club claimed were exorbitant
salary demands in contract
negotiations.

Both Gullit and Vialli
were hugely popular figures
with the fans, as indeed was
Vialli's replacement, fellow
Italian Claudio Ranieri.
Considering that the
silver-haired Ranieri won
precisely nothing during
his four years at the Bridge
this might seem somewhat

strange, especially as the former Napoli, Fiorentina and
Valencia coach struggled to express himself in English
after arriving from Atletico Madrid in 2000. Yet, over
time, the supporters warmed to him, partly because
of the year-by-year improvement in the team's form,
but also because Ranieri conducted himself with great
dignity in his final season when speculation was rife
that new owner Roman Abramovich was about to
replace him with England boss Sven Goran Eriksson.
In the event the bespectacled, bed-hopping Swede
stayed with the national team but, despite leading the
Blues to a creditable second place in the Premiership
in 2004, Ranieri was not spared the axe.

All this might suggest that Chelsea managers,

Ted Drake, pictured
at his desk in 1955,
stayed in the hotseat
for nine years

Coach Dave Sexton and manager Tommy Docherty set out tactics in 1963

regardless of results, can expect to last as long in the job as the average Italian prime minister. And while that may be true in recent decades, Blues bosses of yesteryear were usually given much more time in the role. For instance, Ted Drake, a famous pre-war striker with Arsenal and England, enjoyed a nine-year stint as Chelsea boss after arriving from Reading in 1952. Three years later Drake led the Blues to their first ever league championship, a remarkable achievement given that most of the players in his team had been recruited from the lower leagues or, indeed, non-league football.

Drake's successor, joke-cracking Scot Tommy Docherty, was another to get a fair crack of the whip in the Bridge hotseat. Appointed permanent manager in January 1962 after a three-month trial, 'the Doc' built a young, exciting side, dubbed 'Docherty's Diamonds', who might easily have won much more than just the League Cup in 1965. Docherty's maverick, outspoken style, though, did not always go down well with the Chelsea directors and he was eventually dismissed in October 1967 while under a Football Association suspension for abusive remarks he had made to a local ref on a club tour to the Caribbean.

His replacement, Dave Sexton, was an altogether less colourful character but had already gained a reputation as an outstanding coach during a stint as Docherty's assistant before becoming number one at Leyton Orient. The core of players Sexton inherited was a strong one, including the likes of Peter Bonetti, Charlie Cooke, Ron Harris and Peter Osgood, but over the next seven years he showed his ability in the transfer market by making some inspired signings to perfect the balance he was seeking between steely resolve and creative artistry. The result was a marvellously entertaining and extravagantly gifted Chelsea side which could beat anybody on its day, as it proved by winning the FA Cup and European Cup Winners' Cup in consecutive seasons.

Rather like Sexton, current boss Carlo Ancelotti is not one to seek the limelight, preferring to go about his business in a quiet, relaxed manner. The Italian's approach has worked superbly so far, suggesting he may occupy the Bridge hotseat for some years to come.

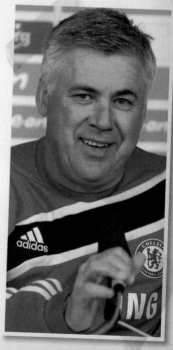

One season, two trophies – not a bad start for Carlo Ancelotti!

MEMORABLE
MATCHES

CHELSEA 2 REAL MADRID 1
European Cup-Winners' Cup Final Replay
Karaiskakis Stadium, Athens, 21st May 1971

A year after winning the FA Cup for the first time in the club's history, Dave Sexton's flamboyant Blues team reached the final of the European Cup Winners' Cup.

Their opponents in Athens were Real Madrid, the most glamorous club side on the continent and winners of the European Cup on a record six occasions.

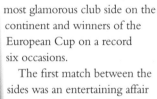

The first match between the sides was an entertaining affair but ended deadlocked after Chelsea defender John Dempsey gifted Real a last-minute equaliser to cancel out Peter Osgood's opener. The replay took place in the same venue two days later.

The Blues dominated from the start and deservedly took the lead on the half hour when Dempsey, atoning for his earlier error in some style, gloriously volleyed home after his header from Charlie Cooke's left-wing corner had only been parried by Real goalkeeper Borja.

Jubilation as Chelsea lift their first European trophy

Minutes later Osgood received the ball from his strike partner Tommy Baldwin and struck a low shot from the edge of the area just inside the post to double Chelsea's lead. It was a typical piece of opportunism from Osgood, and fully vindicated Sexton's decision to play the Blues' talisman despite a nagging knee injury.

Chelsea remained in almost complete control of the game until 15 minutes from the end, when Fleitas pulled a goal back for Real. In the closing stages the Londoners came under increasing pressure, Peter Bonetti diving full length to save Zoco's header and David Webb blocking Amancio almost on the goal line before, joyously for the Blues' players and fans, the final whistle sounded.

Ron Harris stepped up to become the first Chelsea captain to collect a European trophy and was then joined by his jubilant team-mates and dozens of excited supporters on a chaotic lap of honour. While the celebrations continued, Sexton paid tribute to his team.

"We set out to take the initiative," he said, "and here we are with the Cup. Yes, we had to fight for it, but in the end we fought harder than Real. The way our boys never faltered has made me feel proud of them."

Chelsea:
Bonetti; Harris, Dempsey, Webb, Boyle; Weller, Cooke, Hudson, Houseman; Osgood (Smethurst), Baldwin

Scorers:
Dempsey, Osgood

Attendance:
24,000

CHELSEA 5 LEEDS UNITED 0

Division Two, 28th April 1984

After five long years in the Second Division, during which the Blues had even flirted with relegation to the third tier, Chelsea had the chance to clinch promotion back to the top flight when they faced old rivals Leeds United at the Bridge on a gloriously sunny April afternoon.

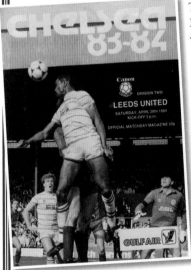

Throughout the season a young Blues team had played with wonderful verve and panache and they put on another vibrant display in front of over 30,000 noisy, shirt-sleeved home fans. Tearing into Leeds right from the start, Chelsea were rewarded with an early goal when left winger Mickey Thomas, an inspired mid-season signing from Stoke, drilled home from close range. Leading scorer Kerry Dixon headed a second, and when the blond-haired striker netted again with a delicate chip from outside the penalty area the match was over as a contest before half-time.

"We want to go up in style," said the programme notes

During the break chairman Ken Bates appeared on the pitch to urge fans to stay off the playing

surface until after the final whistle. The blue hordes heeded the warning when Dixon completed his hat-trick with a wonderful 20-yard volley, but when substitute Paul Canoville raced through a static Leeds defence before lashing the ball into the net in the last minute a mass pitch invasion ensued, during which referee Gilbert Napthine was sent flying.

Thousands more stormed onto the pitch at the end of the game, the Chelsea players beating a hasty retreat down the tunnel before re-emerging, champagne bottles in hand, to throw their shirts into the crowd. Predictably, the constant chants of "Chelsea are back!" and "We're going up, we're going up, you're not!" did not go down well with the Leeds fans on the North Stand terrace who took out their frustrations on the Blues' electronic scoreboard.

Nothing, though, could spoil a truly memorable day for Chelsea, the highpoint of a terrific campaign for the Londoners. "It's one of the best seasons I've had in football," said the Blues' veteran manager John Neal afterwards. "At this time it's the players who deserve the plaudits. They've gone out and done a marvellous job." They certainly had.

Sharpshooter Kerry Dixon bagged a hat-trick

Chelsea:
Niedzwiecki; Lee, Pates, McLaughlin, Jones; Nevin, Bumstead (Canoville), Spackman, Thomas; Dixon, Speedie

Scorers:
Thomas, Dixon 3, Canoville

Attendance:
33,447

CHELSEA 4 LIVERPOOL 2
FA Cup fourth round, 26th January 1997

For sheer drama and edge-of-the-seat excitement, few games in Chelsea history can match this epic FA Cup tie between Ruud Gullit's 'Lovely Boys' and Liverpool.

The big talking point before kick-off was the recall of Gianluca Vialli, making his first start in six weeks during a difficult first season at the Bridge. The Italian striker, though, was a marginal figure in the first half as the visitors took a vice-like grip on the game with two early goals by Robbie Fowler and Stan Collymore. It could have been worse for the Blues, too, as Steve McManaman missed a gilt-edged chance shortly before the break.

Recalling Gianluca Vialli paid off handsomely

At half-time, veterans of Chelsea's 1955 title-winning side were introduced to the fans. "Bring them on!" chanted the crowd, seemingly resigned to defeat. The mood rapidly changed, though, when substitute Mark Hughes pulled a goal back five minutes into the second half, turning sharply to squeeze a low shot past David James.

Suddenly Liverpool, so slick and composed before, appeared flustered. Minutes later the Blues were level, Hughes laying the ball off for Gianfranco Zola to unleash a blistering left-foot shot into the top corner. Chelsea now had the upper hand and, urged on by the home fans, continued to lay siege to the Reds' goal.

The Blues' next offensive epitomised their breathtaking attacking play since the break, Dan Petrescu collecting Zola's pass before threading a perfect through ball to Vialli, who jabbed a low shot beneath James's dive. It was Vialli, too, who delivered the coup de grace, rising unchallenged to bury Zola's free-kick with a flick of his bald head. Fifteen minutes later the final whistle blew on one of the Blues' greatest comebacks ever, signalling memorable scenes of celebration on the pitch and in the stands.

"I will remember this match for a long time," a thrilled Vialli said afterwards. "We put on the pitch all our capacity, our quality and our art. Our second half was unbelievable!" Even better, the Blues went on to lift the cup at Wembley a few months later, bringing to an end a trophy drought which stretched back 26 years.

Gullit's programme notes praised the team's spirit

Chelsea:
Hitchcock;
Sinclair, Leboeuf,
Clarke, Minto
(M. Hughes);
Petrescu,
Newton, Di
Matteo, Wise;
Zola, Vialli

Scorers:
M. Hughes, Zola,
Vialli 2

Attendance:
27,950

CHELSEA 4 BARCELONA 2

Champions League round of 16, second leg, 8th March 2005

An extraordinary Champions League tie began with the Blues going down to a 2-1 defeat in Barcelona, the Londoners failing to hold on to a first half lead after striker Didier Drogba was sent off.

The suggestion by Chelsea boss Jose Mourinho that Swedish referee Anders Frisk had been influenced in the Catalans' favour by a half-time discussion with Barca manager Frank Rijkaard had caused a huge storm, the controversy filling the sports pages during the two-week gap between the two legs. The stage was set for an epic clash in the return at the Bridge and, for once, events on the pitch more than lived up to the pre-match hype.

From the very first whistle Chelsea ripped into Barcelona, the Blues winning every loose ball before launching fast-paced raids deep into the visitors' territory. Barca looked nervous, and became even more rattled when Eidur Gudjohnsen coolly converted Mateja Kezman's cross after just eight minutes. Frank Lampard soon made it two, tapping into an empty net after Barca goalkeeper Victor Valdes could only parry Joe Cole's deflected shot, and when Damien Duff confidently slotted home Cole's defence-splitting pass the Blues were 3-0 up with only 19 minutes on the clock.

The tie appeared to be in the bag, but Barcelona gradually recovered from their horrendous start and clawed their way back into contention when Ronaldinho converted a penalty awarded against Paulo Ferreira for handball. Then, shortly before half-time, the buck-toothed Brazilian levelled the aggregate score with a marvellous piece of improvisation, curling the ball past Petr Cech with an audacious 20-yard toe poke.

Both sides had further chances to score in the second half, but as the minutes ticked away Chelsea knew they had to net again to avoid going out on the away goals rule. With just 14 minutes left the Blues got the goal they were desperately seeking, skipper John Terry rising high to head in Duff's corner from the left for what proved to be the winner.

"The game was magnificent, unbelievably emotional," said a delighted Mourinho afterwards. "It was changing faces every five minutes. This is a game to the last second."

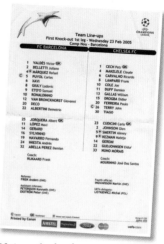

Chelsea:
Cech; Ferreira (Johnson), Terry, Carvalho, Gallas; Cole, Makelele, Lampard, Duff (Huth); Gudjohnsen (Tiago), Kezman

Scorers:
Gudjohnsen, Lampard, Duff, Terry

Attendance:
41,515

CHELSEA COMIC STRIP HISTORY 4

ON 27TH DECEMBER 1971 A GOALKEEPING CRISIS FORCED THE BLUES TO PLAY DEFENDER DAVID WEBB IN GOAL FOR THE WHOLE GAME AGAINST IPSWICH...

DON'T FORGET YOUR GLOVES...

BEFORE THE KICK-OFF, JOKER WEBB KNELT DOWN TO PRAY IN FRONT OF THE SHED...

HIS PRAYERS WERE ANSWERED... HE KEPT THE IPSWICH ATTACK AT BAY, AND CHELSEA WON THE GAME 2-0 !

STORY OF THE BLUES
THE PREMIERSHIP YEARS
1992-2010

Although it's now the richest and most popular league in the world, there was little evidence of glitz and glamour when the Premiership era kicked off at Stadium Bridge in August 1992, a Chelsea team composed entirely of British players drawing 1-1 with Oldham in front of a half-empty stadium.

A disappointing initial campaign in the new league saw boss Ian Porterfield become the first Premiership manager to lose his job, David Webb taking over in a caretaker role in the remaining three months of the season. There was better news in the boardroom, however, as chairman Ken Bates signed a 20-year lease with new landlords the Royal Bank of Scotland to ensure Chelsea's future at the Bridge after a decade-long fight. The agreement paved the way for the development of the ground in the following years, spanking new stands replacing the old dilapidated terraces while flats, hotels, bars and restaurants sprouted outside the stadium as Bates's vision of a multi-purpose 'Chelsea Village' complex was finally realised.

Back on the pitch, in 1994 Chelsea reached their first major cup final for 22 years under new manager Glenn Hoddle. Unfortunately, it was hardly a day to remember as the Blues were thrashed 4-0 in the FA Cup final by Manchester United. Still, just making the final guaranteed European football at the Bridge for the first time in a generation the following season and Hoddle's team gave a good account of

themselves, reaching the semi-finals of the Cup
Winners' Cup before falling to Zaragoza.

The summer of 1995 saw Chelsea recruit their
first big-name foreigner, Dutch maestro and onetime
World Player of the Year Ruud Gullit joining the club
on a free transfer from Sampdoria, former Manchester
United striker Mark Hughes and Romanian wing-
back Dan Petrescu soon following him to the Bridge.
With Gullit pulling the strings, the Blues were a joy
to watch although an FA Cup semi-final defeat to
Manchester United in 1996 was the nearest they got
to silverware.

The long wait for a trophy was finally ended
the following season with a 2-0 victory over
Middlesbrough in the FA Cup final. By now Gullit

Manager Glenn Hoddle
brought in world class
stars such as Mark
Hughes and Ruud Gullit

had succeeded Hoddle as manager and the team he
sent out at Wembley featured a mix of longserving
stalwarts like skipper Dennis Wise and defender Steve
Clarke, along with overseas stars such as the Italian trio
Gianfranco Zola, Gianluca Vialli and Roberto

di Matteo, and French central defender Frank Leboeuf.

Halfway through the next season Gullit was sensationally sacked after contract negotiations with the club broke down, to be replaced as player-manager by Vialli. It proved to be an inspired choice as, within a couple of months, the new boss led the club to triumphs in the Coca-Cola Cup and the European Cup Winners' Cup, Zola coming off the bench to score a spectacular winning goal in the second of these finals against Stuttgart in Stockholm.

Chelsea's 'foreign policy' continued to pay dividends with the Blues qualifying for the Champions League for the first time in 1999 and winning the FA Cup again a year later after a 1-0 defeat of Aston Villa. The cup triumph, though, was not enough to save Vialli from the chop, as a poor start to the 2000/01 season and rumours of dressing room discontent led to his replacement by another Italian, Claudio Ranieri.

Dubbed 'The Tinkerman' by the press for

Celebratiuons in Stockholm after Chelsea beat VFB Stuttgart 1-0 to lift the 1998 Cup Winners' Cup

his constant changes in team selection and tactics,
Nonetheless, Ranieri led the Blues to the FA Cup
final in his first full season in charge and a Champions
League place the following year despite a financial
crisis at the club which severely limited his options in
the transfer market.

Such constraints became a thing of the past, though,
when Russian billionaire Roman Abramovich bought
the club from Bates in the summer of 2003. The

Blues immediately went on a massive spending spree, splashing out in excess of £100 million on the likes of Joe Cole, Damien Duff and Claude Makelele. The new team were the talk of world football but, despite a second-place finish in the Premiership and an impressive Champions League campaign which was eventually halted by Monaco in the semi-finals, the Blues' failure to land a trophy cost Ranieri his job.

His replacement was the charismatic Jose

Not only a first League title in 50 years but the Carling Cup too - no wonder the fans are overjoyed

Mourinho, manager of Champions League winners Porto. After announcing in his first press conference that he was 'a special one', Mourinho lived up to his own billing by creating a highly competitive and tactically flexible team which proved exceptionally difficult to beat. Reinforced by the likes of Petr Cech, Didier Drogba and Ricardo Carvalho, the Blues swept to the Premiership title, two goals by Frank Lampard wrapping up the championship on a memorable afternoon at Bolton. For good measure, skipper John Terry also got his hands on the Carling Cup, the Blues defeating Liverpool 3-2 in an exciting final in Cardiff.

The following season Chelsea retained their title in imperious style, clinching the championship with a 3-0 humbling of closest challengers Manchester United at a jubilant Stamford Bridge. The cash-rich Blues were widely tipped to make it a treble but, despite signing two star names in Andrei Shevchenko and Michael Ballack, had to settle for second place behind United in 2007, although success in both the Carling Cup and the FA Cup provided some consolation.

Behind the scenes, though, all was not well. The deterioration in the relationship between Abramovich and Mourinho led to the latter leaving the club in September 2007. The Blues battled on regardless, reaching the Champions League final before losing unluckily to United on penalties in Moscow. That setback saw the end of Mourinho's replacement, Israeli coach Avram Grant, and the arrival of Luiz Felipe Scolari, who had guided Brazil to the World Cup some six years earlier in 2002. After an encouraging start, however, the Brazilian was found wanting in the Premiership and in February 2009, following a series of decidedly lacklustre performances by his team, became the fourth manager to be shown the door by Abramovich.

For the remainder of the season Chelsea were managed by the experienced Dutch coach Guus Hiddink on a temporary basis before he returned to his job with the Russian national team. He did remarkably well given the circumstances, guiding the Blues to the semi-finals of the Champions League and an FA Cup final triumph against Everton before handing over the reins to another manager with a hugely impressive CV, former AC Milan boss Carlo Ancelotti. The Italian enjoyed a superb first season at the club, guiding the Blues to a first ever league and cup Double. The only blot on his copybook was a disappointingly early Champions League exit but, as the silverware piled up, that was soon forgotten.

JT and Frank Lampard celebrate winning the 2010 FA Cup to secure Chelsea's first ever Double

THE QUEST FOR THE CHAMPIONS LEAGUE

In the history of the Champions League no club that has yet to lift the trophy has been as close on so many occasions to winning the competition as Chelsea. Even more gallingly, the Blues have enjoyed no luck at all in the knock-out stages of the tournament, frequently being eliminated in circumstances which even neutrals would admit were extremely unfortunate or, in some cases, grossly unfair.

Chelsea have been chasing their Champions League dream since the 1999/2000 season when the club competed in the competition for the first time, but the Blues could easily have made their debut in the tournament's predecessor, the European Cup, as far back as 1955. As English league champions the club were invited to take part in the first edition of the competition but under pressure from the FA, who were concerned about the possible impact on domestic attendances and were generally suspicious about 'foreign' initiatives, declined to participate.

When the Blues eventually qualified for the Champions League, in 1999 under manager Gianluca Vialli, they more than made up for lost time. A 5-0 thrashing of Galatasaray in front of their own fanatical supporters was the highlight of the two group stages before the Blues met Barcelona in a mouth-watering quarter-final. On one of the great European nights at the Bridge, Chelsea beat the Catalan giants 3-1 but were unable to hang onto their two-goal advantage in the Nou Camp, going down 5-1 after extra time.

After a three-year gap a revamped Blues team, bankrolled by new owner Roman Abramovich's millions, returned to the Champions League in 2003. A stunning 4-0 win away to Lazio helped Chelsea top their group before Stuttgart were narrowly seen off in the last 16. In the quarter-finals

The trophy with the big ears continues to elude the club

the Blues famously got the better of arch rivals Arsenal, full back Wayne Bridge scoring a memorable winner at Highbury that is still celebrated in song by the Chelsea faithful to this day. The semi-final against Monaco looked eminently winnable but, hindered by some bizarre tactical decisions by manager Claudio Ranieri, the Blues lost 3-1 in the first leg and were knocked out after a 2-2 draw back at the Bridge.

There was more heartache for Chelsea at the semi-final stage the following season, despite the acquisition of Porto's Champions League-winning manager, Jose Mourinho. After exciting wins against Barcelona and Bayern Munich in the previous rounds the Blues were strong favourites to beat Liverpool in the last four. However, following a dull stalemate at the Bridge, the Merseysiders went through to the final thanks to Luis Garcia's controversial goal in the return at Anfield. Chelsea claims that the ball had not crossed the line appeared to be backed up by TV replays, a furious Mourinho insisting that his team had been beaten by "a ghost goal".

A year later the Blues paid the price for not winning their group when they were drawn against Barcelona in the first knock-out round. Again there was controversy as Chelsea went down to a 2-1 home defeat in the first leg, Mourinho claiming that left back Asier Del Horno was unjustly dismissed for a foul on tricky Barca winger Lionel Messi. A two-goal victory in the Nou Camp never seemed likely, the Blues going out rather tamely following a 1-1 draw.

Another year, another opportunity. For the third time the Blues reached the semi-finals in 2007, after close-run victories against Porto and Valencia in the earlier knock-out stages. Again, Liverpool blocked Chelsea's route to the final, but a single goal by Joe Cole put the Blues in good heart for the Anfield return.

The visitors' lead didn't last long, Daniel Agger soon levelling the scores, but there were no further strikes in the rest of the match or in extra-time. Sadly, the Blues' luck was out in the penalty shoot-out, with Liverpool winning easily.

As every Chelsea fan knows, the following season provided more pain when the Blues lost in the final to Manchester United on penalties in Moscow, John Terry slipping and putting his spot-kick just wide when the trophy was within the skipper's grasp. That appeared to be the last word in devastating Champions League defeats, until Barcelona piled on yet more agony in the 2009 semi-final. Iniesta wielded the dagger with a last-minute away goals decider at the Bridge, but that killer blow would have been a mere pinprick if the Norwegian referee had not turned down no fewer than four strong Chelsea penalty appeals.

The Blues had fewer complaints about their elimination by Mourinho's Inter Milan in the last 16 the following year, although Saloman Kalou was denied a clear penalty in the first leg in Italy. The defeat left Chelsea fans reflecting on a decade of bitter disappointments in the Champions League and hoping for better luck in the future.

HONOURS AND RECORDS

MAJOR HONOURS
WINNERS
Football League 1955
Premier League 2005, 2006, 2010
Football League Division Two 1984, 1989
FA Cup 1970, 1997, 2000, 2007, 2009, 2010
League Cup 1965, 1998, 2005, 2007
European Cup-Winners' Cup 1971, 1998
European Super Cup 1998

RUNNERS-UP
Premier League 2004, 2007, 2008
Football League Division Two 1907, 1912, 1930, 1963, 1977
FA Cup 1915, 1967, 1994, 2002
Football League Cup 1972, 2008
Champions League 2008

MINOR HONOURS
Football League South Cup 1945

Charity/Community Shield 1955, 2000, 2005, 2009
Full Members Cup 1986, 1990

RUNNERS-UP
Football League South Cup 1944
Charity/Community Shield 1970, 1997, 2006, 2007

RECORDS
FOOTBALL LEAGUE/PREMIER LEAGUE RECORDS
- Chelsea's goal difference of +71 in 2009/10 is a record for the top flight of English football.
- In the 2004/05 season Chelsea conceded just 15 league goals, a record for all divisions of the Football League and Premiership.
- Between 20th March 2004 and 26th October 2008 Chelsea were unbeaten at home for 86 league games, a record for all divisions of

the Football League and Premiership.

- Between 5th April 2008 and 6th December 2008 Chelsea won 11 consecutive away games, a record for all divisions of the Football League and Premiership.
- **Chelsea's total of 95 points in 2004/05 is a record for the top flight of English football.**

PREMIER LEAGUE RECORDS

- **In 2009/10 Chelsea scored a Premiership record 103 goals.**
- In both 2004/05 and 2005/06 Chelsea won a record 29 Premiership matches.
- **In 2005/06 Chelsea won a record 18 of 19 home matches in the Premiership.**
- In 2004/05 Chelsea had 25 clean sheets in 38 matches, a record for the Premiership.

CLUB RECORDS

- Most points in a league season: 99, Division Two, 1988/89
- **Most league wins in a season: 29, 1988/89, 2004/05 and 2005/06**
- Most consecutive league wins: 10, 19th November 2005-15th January 2006
- **Most consecutive home league wins: 13, 26th November 1910-22nd April 1911 and 23rd April 2005-31st December 2005**
- Most consecutive away league wins: 11, 5th April 2008-6th December 2008
- **Most league goals in a season: 103, 2009/10**

- Most home league goals in a season: 68, 2009/10
- **Most away league goals in a season: 46, 1988/89**
- Record win: Chelsea 13 Jeunesse Hautcharage 0, 29th September 1971
- **Record league win: Chelsea 8 Wigan Athletic 0, 9th May 2010**
- Record defeat: Wolverhampton Wanderers 8 Chelsea 1, 26th September 1953

INDIVIDUAL RECORDS

- Most appearances (total): 795, Ron Harris (1962-80)
- **Most appearances (league): 655, Ron Harris (1962-80)**
- Most goals (total): 202, Bobby Tambling (1959-69)
- **Most goals (league): 164, Bobby Tambling (1959-64)**
- Most goals in a season (total): 43, Jimmy Greaves, 1960/61
- **Most goals in a season (league): 41, Jimmy Greaves, 1960/61**
- Most hat-tricks: 13, Jimmy Greaves, 1957-61
- **Oldest player: Dickie Spence, 39 years and 57 days, 13th September 1947**
- Youngest player: Ian 'Chico' Hamilton, 16 years and 138 days, 18th March 1967
- **Oldest goalscorer: Dickie Spence, 38 years and 282 days, 26th April 1947**
- Youngest goalscorer: Ian 'Chico' Hamilton, 16 years and 138 days, 18th March 1967

- Consecutive league appearances: Frank Lampard, 164, 13th October 2001-26th December 2005
- Most expensive signing: Andriy Shevchenko, £30 million from AC Milan, May 2006
- **Record sale: Arjen Robben, £24 million to Real Madrid, July 2007**

ATTENDANCE RECORDS AT STAMFORD BRIDGE

- Highest attendance: 100,000 (estimated), Chelsea v Moscow Dynamo, 13th November 1945

- Highest league attendance: 82,905, Chelsea v Arsenal, 12th October 1935
- Highest average league attendance: 48,302, 1954/55
- **Highest FA Cup attendance: 77,952, Chelsea v Swindon Town, 13th March 1913**
- Highest League Cup attendance: 43,330, Chelsea v Tottenham Hotspur, 22nd December 1971
- **Highest European attendance: 59,541, Chelsea v AC Milan, Fairs Cup, 16th February 1966**
- Lowest attendance: 3,000, Chelsea v Lincoln City, 17th February 1906
- **Lowest average league attendance: 12,737, 1982/83**

FA CUP RECORDS

- Biggest FA Cup win: Chelsea 9 Worksop Town 1, 11th January 1908
- **Most FA Cup appearances: 64, Ron Harris (left) (1964-80)**
- Most FA Cup goals: 25, Bobby Tambling (1962-69)
- **Most goals in a single FA Cup match: 6, George Hilsdon v Worksop Town, 11th January 1908**
- Most FA Cup goals in a season: 8, Peter Osgood, 1970
- **Record FA Cup defeat: Crystal Palace 7 Chelsea 1, 18th November 1905**

LEAGUE CUP RECORDS

- Biggest League Cup win: Doncaster Rovers 0 Chelsea 7, 16th November 1960
- **Most League Cup appearances:**

48, John Hollins (1963-74 and 1983) and Ron Harris (1963-79)
- Most League Cup goals: 25, Kerry Dixon (1983-91)
- **Most goals in a single League Cup match: 4, Kerry Dixon v Gillingham, 13th September 1983**
- Most League Cup goals in a season: 8, Kerry Dixon, 1984/85
- **Record League Cup defeat: Stoke City 6 Chelsea 2, 22nd October 1974**

EUROPEAN RECORDS
- **Biggest European win: Chelsea 13 Jeunesse Hautcharage 0, European Cup Winners' Cup, 29th September 1971 (the aggregate score of 21-0 is a European record).**
- Most European appearances: 80 Frank Lampard, 2001-
- **Most European goals: 26 Didier Drogba, 2004-**
- Most goals in a single European match: 5, Peter Osgood v Jeunesse Hautcharage, 29th September 1971
- **Most European goals in a season: 8, Tore Andre Flo, Champions League, 1999/2000**
- Record European defeat: Barcelona 5 Chelsea 0, Fairs Cup, 25th May 1966

FIRSTS AND LASTS
- In 2010 Chelsea's Ashley Cole became the first player to win the FA Cup six times (including three victories with Arsenal).
- Chelsea were the last club to win the FA Cup at the old Wembley stadium, beating Aston Villa 1-0 in the final in 2000.
- **Along with Arsenal, Chelsea were the first club to wear shirt numbers, sporting them for their Second Division fixture against Swansea Town on 25th August 1928.**
- Chelsea were the first club to win the FA Cup at the new Wembley stadium, beating Manchester United 1-0 after extra-time in the final in 2007.
- **On 27th January 1974 Chelsea, along with Stoke City, became the first English club to play a Football League First Division fixture on a Sunday.**
- On 26th December 1999 at Southampton, Chelsea became the first English club to field a starting line-up entirely made up of players born outside the United Kingdom.
- **Chelsea were the last English club to win the European Cup-Winners' Cup in 1998 and, the following year, the last English club to compete in the tournament before it was scrapped by UEFA.**
- In 1955 Chelsea were the first English club to be invited to take part in the European Cup, but declined the offer under pressure from the FA.
- **Chelsea striker Peter Osgood is the last player to have scored in every round of the FA Cup, achieving this feat in 1970.**